Conversations With Collies

D1421526

JAY GURDEN

Copyright © 2019 by Jay Gurden

All rights reserved. No part of this book
may be reproduced or used in any
manner without the written permission
of the copyright owner except for the
use of quotations in a book review.

ISBN13: 978-1-7946-6599-6
ISBN10: 1-7946-6599-4

CONTENTS

Introduction   i

Dramatis Canidae   1

What a girl wants   11

Motherly love?   14

Renaissance Dog   17

Taking the direct route   21

A sense of purpose   24

Toying with Tiggywinkle   27

An excitation of anticipation   29

Showing some enthusiasm   31

Wicked Woof of the West?   33

Not what I meant by dietary fibre!   35

Shook up by snowfall   37

Funny interpretation of friendly   40

A rowdy rodent   44

Less Casanova, more casa NO THANKS!   46

Not so much brotherly love   49

Over the top   52

The single minded sheepdog 55

A chivalrous collie dog 58

Different kind of food run 62

A boundless ball of enthusiasm 64

Ducking the issue 67

Snow queen 70

Centre of (in)attention 72

Conniving cows 74

The treatment he deserves 77

Hoarder collie 80

Pavements are for dogs! 83

Abandoned in company 86

Big is better! 89

CPS - Collie Positioning System 92

Quirky canine 94

Garden warfare 97

Practical priorities 99

Sweltering summer snuggles 101

Purloined by a puppy 104

Pooch with poise 107

The evolution of a species 110

Red lorry, yellow lorry. No, Red's lorry 112

If you can't stand the heat 115

Puppy protection inc. 117

A dog's got to do… 119

Patience brings rewards 121

Whose bed? 123

Distraction in action 127

Its vision is based on movement 129

How to win friends etc 131

About the author 134

INTRODUCTION

"If only I could know what they're thinking!"

This is a common thought for those of us who share our lives with animals. Most of us have at some point looked at our pets and wished that they could tell us how they feel, or their opinions on what is going on in their lives. I know it is something that I have thought more than once.

Then I started to think about some of the dogs who have been in my life. Each of them has been a wonderful dog in a number of ways, much loved and, in the cases of those we have lost, much missed. Our breed of choice here is the Border Collie, renowned for their intelligence and quick brains. The more I thought about it, the more I began to wonder whether I did really want to know what some of them thought about me!

The idea simply would not let go, however, and this book is the result. Contained within is a collection of humorous remembrances, of actual events that have happened in my history with dogs. They appear in no particular order and do not follow any kind of timeline. What they all have in common is the inclusion of the canine side of the conversation, interpreted from what I know of each dog's personality. I have discovered that Border Collies may have a natural flair for sarcasm, and are not always impressed with the human intellect, but are happy to give their opinions freely.

In short - Conversations with Collies.

DRAMATIS CANIDAE (PLUS A MINION)

Here is a little more information about the stars of this book – the dogs. They are all real dogs that have been in my life at some point, and the conversations are interpretations of what they might have said at the time, based on memories of real events that happened.

Cass

I first met Cass when she was about twelve weeks old. She belonged to a man that some of my friends thought would be a good match for me. Considering that, at the time of writing, we have been married for twenty years at some point I am going to have to admit they were right.

Unlike most dogs that have a long name but suit their short name far more, there were times when Cass most definitely suited Cassandra better. Fiercely independent and the possessor of very strong opinions, she was an amazing dog to have if she was in the frame of mind to work with you. On the days she was being a little more... self-opinionated, there was little to do but wait her out, as once she had done what she wanted to do, she would then come back and do whatever you needed her to.

It would only ever take a few minutes of being with Cass to get the feeling that this incredibly intelligent dog was judging you, and judging you hard. For a ball or a biscuit, she would forgive you your shortcomings, at least for a little while. She was not a dog that craved or asked for a lot of fuss, so on the rare occasions that she would come to me for a cuddle I would feel immensely privileged. That feeling would persist until the next time she would look at me with an expression that said perfectly without words that she clearly considered me an idiot.

Life with Cass was never what you could consider boring, as she had a range of methods to ensure she kept us on our toes. She left us at the age of eleven when something caused her suddenly to lose the use of her hind end one day. Such a huge character left a massive void, and she remains very close to our hearts, even many years later and we frequently reminisce about some of the events that occurred with her, many of which are included in this book.

Dillan

Following Cass came Dillan, one of the puppies from the first of two litters we bred from Cass.

Dillan was not even the puppy that I first intended to keep from the litter, having instead picked out a big male tricolour puppy to keep, but people coming to pick the puppy they wanted to take home when they reached eight weeks old repeatedly overlooked the little tricolour bitch. She had quite a bit of white on her face and one blue eye, which seemed to disturb people. I spent a lot of her lifetime, when out with her among people, answering the question of whether she was blind in that eye because of the colour. Once I had taken the decision to keep her and put in more one on one time with her, I was quickly enamoured.

Dillan was quite simply one of the most loving dogs I have ever encountered. She adored people and loved nothing more than cuddling up given the chance. In that, she was the complete opposite of her mother. That was also the case when it came to intelligence; if ever I thought that all Border Collies had phenomenal intelligence, Dillan disabused me of that notion from a very early age. She was very easy to be around, had a fantastic temperament and was incredibly biddable. I think just about anyone would have been able to work with her, as she loved to work and would take any opportunity. She was just... not bright. At all.

One of the daftest habits she had, that we could never get her to stop, was chasing the wheels of the Land Rover, darting from one side to the other just in front of the wheels, as we would drive across the fields checking the sheep. One day she cut it too close and the almost inevitable happened. Both front and rear wheels went over her. I was not there on that day but came home to an answering machine message that Dillan was at the vet's surgery. She was remarkable lucky with her injuries really, although her dislocated hip would not go back in and so the end of the bone was removed. She spent a year on three legs before she would try standing on the fourth leg, the first few months of that year spent just riding around in the farm truck and watching Cass work. After some time spent getting fit again, it became hard to notice that anything had happened, although when tired she would move both hind legs together as one.

When we left the farm, Dillan went to live on another farm with my father in law. As she loved any people and definitely loved the farm life, she settled in there very well. When she finally departed, at the age of thirteen, she did so in the most Dillan way possible. One morning she simply did not come out of the kennel for her breakfast, having gone in her sleep. Her tail was still tucked across her nose, just as she would sleep. Dillan was definitely the sweetest natured of the dogs in my personal canine history.

Red

Red was a beautiful blue merle. He was called Red for precisely this reason – my husband proclaimed when we were puppy hunting that if we came home with a red coloured puppy they would be called Blue, and a blue puppy would be called Red. I am not entirely sure why I let him decide names as he also said that if we bought a bitch, she would be called Dog. Red was the last dog that we selected with working sheep in mind as we sold up and moved out of farming when he was two years old. He made his position on working clear very early on in his life, and took up a serious position as chief tennis ball chaser and escort to my mother when she would go running out of the house to watch the huge military Chinook helicopters that would regularly fly over the farm. He liked fuss at home on his own terms but out in public loved anybody and everybody that wanted to say hi to him.

As we moved on from the farm and my husband made the transition to driving an HGV, Red became his lorry dog. He again took these duties very seriously, with excellent performance in supervising loading and unloading, patrolling the yard while dodging the forklift, with an ever-present tennis ball in his mouth. He succeeded in training just about all of the people working for the company to throw the ball for him on demand, and fetch it if it went somewhere he did not want to try and get to. He also aced the task of crashing out on the bed in the back of the cab and snoring loudly (although would always deny that he had ever fallen asleep if caught).

I called Red my opinionated, complicated, grumpy old man as he was not a fan of being groomed or doing anything he deemed unnecessary (a lingering issue from an illness as an adolescent that required regular medication for a while). In some ways, he was the easiest dog ever. As a young dog, he very rarely left the farm in his first few months, except to go to vets appointments or on a few visits to family. As he hit around eight months, the sheep showing season started, and he came round the circuit of shows in which we took part. He was a dog that we could take anywhere without a second thought and would sit or lay quietly when needed, or happily walk around and interact with anyone that wanted to say hi. I have a distinct memory of taking him to one event a few miles from home. My husband had gone into a building where dogs were not allowed and we waited for him outside. While we were standing there, something like thirty people must have come out of the building and walked past us. He looked at every single one of them and wagged his tail, yet not even one fussed him or even acknowledged him. He looked so forlorn until we started moving again.

Red lived to the age of fourteen and a half and we only lost him a few months before I started writing this book. It is still a huge loss, one that is very capable of catching me out. Such a huge personality meant that for weeks I could have sworn I saw him out of the corner of my eye and kept expecting to find him in his accustomed sleeping place at the bottom of the stairs or peeping at me around the door between the hall and sitting room. He could be tetchy, quirky, and difficult to handle for things like grooming, but despite that, he was a beautiful dog, inside and out.

Finn

How do I begin to describe my crazy, chaotic, loving, beautiful blue merle boy?

Although when the time came to find another dog we had already left the farm and had no need of a working dog, we still went looking at working bred Border Collies. They are what we know and are used to, and we really like their brains and personalities. Our trip to collect our puppy took us from one side of the country to the other, Brighton on the south-east coast of England to Cardiff, a distance of pretty much two hundred miles each way. Strangely enough, he has never had much of a problem with car travel with the journey home as his first major trip!

As Finn grew, it started to become apparent that he was not like the dogs we have had before. Due to illness, he did not get out and about in the way that we had planned to do with him, and he started to get ever more shy of other dogs and people that he did not know. He became fearful of new things he had not encountered before and would spend a lot of time on his walks in a state of anxious anticipation, looking for things to be worried about.

Life with Finn has never been what could be called easy, and there are restrictions on our lives now because we cannot simply leave him with someone else to look after him for the day, as we could with previous dogs. His world that he is comfortable with is very small and, while we are working to improve that, the nature of his fears means that progress steps are small and we have to be very careful that he is not surprised by people he does not know, for instance.

With a lot of hard work, study and support from some wonderfully knowledgeable people, we are starting to be able to expand his world again. It is very hard work and can be very stressful for the people that are living with him, but because of this madcap bundle of fur, ears and fun, I have discovered a whole new group of people and an entirely new career.

I am conscious that, when describing Finn, it appears that everything is very negative. For the people that he knows and trusts, Finn is the most loving, demonstrative and adorable dog that you could possibly imagine. He is a dog that loves contact and is at his happiest chilling on the sofa using a human as a pillow or cuddling up in front of the TV. He adores learning new tricks and is very bright, making him incredibly rewarding to work with.

Rhody (Roo)

Roo was a little bit of an interloper in the metaphorical pack, as she was not a Border Collie and did not belong to me. She was, in fact, a Jack Russell, formerly belonging to my nephew, but later in her life ruling the house in which my mother and sister live. While she may have been small in stature, she was very definitely not small in character, and in her own mind was probably at least the size of a Great Dane. She had far too much character and influence in our lives not to be included and was a particular friend of Red's throughout the time that she lived with Mum and my sister. She was a bit less sure of Finn sometimes, because he is enormous and quite bouncy (and sometimes rather possessive of 'his' people), and she was a genteel little old lady by the time he joined the clan. Roo very sadly left the family while I was in the process of writing this book, and will be much missed, leaving a gap much larger than a Jack Russell in all of our lives in the process.

The minion (me!)

(The picture is very clearly not me, but I love this little

character so much!)

My name is Jay, as per the cover of this book, although I also on social media go by the name Blue Merle Minion in a few places. In 2018, I started a blog with this title. In the beginning, it shared the comedies and dramas of living with two blue merle canine clowns. As time went on and Finn's fearfulness and anxiety prompted me to study canine behaviour, the focus of the blog switched to training, behaviour, and supporting other owners that found themselves in the same position as me. No longer a farmer, I spent a number of years as a laboratory technician for a biotechnology company. When the company was sold, I was made redundant. It was after this that Finn came into our lives, and I was able to dedicate a lot of time to study. Now, I spend most of my time split between collie cuddling, continuing my studies and writing, both as a freelance content writer and as an author.

.

WHAT A GIRL WANTS

Dillan was generally a very easy dog to have around in all ways, meaning we could take her anywhere with us, and usually did.

Me: "County show time, Dillan. Let's have a nice day wandering around the showground, eat some bad for us stuff and see what we can find to look at."
Dillan: "I zoned out after the mention of food. Look, there's an ice-cream van."
Me: "It's nine in the morning. We can get ice cream later. We might find a bacon roll or a burger in a while."
Dillan: "I suppose, Hey, what's going on in that ring over there?"
Me: "Looks like there are some Gurkhas over there. Let's go and see."

We make our way over and find a seat on a bench, the front row of three right by the side of the ring. It becomes clear on looking closer that this is the Band of the Brigade of Gurkhas about to begin a musical formation marching display. I sit Dillan down between my ankles to avoid her bothering people either side for fuss. The music begins right next to where we are sitting and I am enthralled until someone taps me on the shoulder. Turning around, I see it is the person in the row behind me.

Person: "The man behind me wants a word."
Man: "Uh, is this your dog?"
Dillan: "LOUD!"
Me: "Sorry Dillan, I didn't think you'd be that scared, and didn't realise you'd shot backwards."
Dillan: "LOUD!"
Me: "Ok, let's go and find that burger to share and then we can walk around some more where it's not quite so noisy."

We go and find the quietest corner we can manage, and have something to eat while Dillan gets over her fright and calms back down. Once she seems back to her normal self, we start walking around again.

Dillan: "Is that a buggy?"
Me: "That over there? Yes, it is."
Dillan: "Does it have a baby in it?"
Me: "Possibly. That is what they're for."
Dillan: "We're going over there."
Me: "You know I'm not a huge fan of babies."
Dillan: "Don't care. We are going over there."

Although a physically small example of a Border Collie bitch, she tows me over to greet the small child. The parents are understandably a little concerned by the dog bearing down on their child until I explain that

Dillan adores small children and just wants to say hi. She is permitted to say hello and then we move along.

Dillan: "Look, there's a small child walking over there!"
Me: "Really? We just did the saying hello to a child thing!"
Dillan: "Oh, he's seen me and wants to say hello. Let's go."
Me: "I guess we can say hello to one more and that's it."

We go and say hi to that child and then continue on our way.

Dillan: "Look! There's another buggy!"

I think we greeted almost every baby and young child on the showground that day. As unenthusiastic as I was about so many small people, Dillan could never get enough of kids. I have never known another dog that so actively adored children.

MOTHERLY LOVE?

Years ago, when we were living on farms and had our own flock of sheep, we bred a couple of litters of puppies from Cass. The second litter consisted of two puppies and did not really leave much in the way of lasting memories. Her first litter contained eight puppies, one of whom grew up into our next working sheepdog, Dillan. Cass was at times more of a dutiful mother than an enthusiastic one and definitely felt that she benefited from regular breaks away from the puppies, coming out for short walks with us.

Me: "Stay up here for now, Cass. It will only take me a few minutes to call the girls up, so you may as well stay quiet with the pups.
Cass: "Are you sure you don't need me? Where are you going?"

I leave her where she is and head out to the field.

Me: "Right sheep, you need to behave. It's still going to be a little while longer yet before Cass is back to work. Here. Follow me with this bucket of yummy sheep food."

Just before I turn back around to start making my way in the direction of the barn, the sheep scatter away from me even as I'm trying to get them to follow me. I become aware of a rapidly approaching loud clapping sound.

Cass: "I'm here! I'm here! I'll get these sheep in for you, really quick."
Me: "What on earth is that weird noise?"
Cass: "Hey, lay off me. I can't help the fact that I'm lactating, and they flap around and clap together when I run."
Me: "Wow... Ok, I suppose if you're here and comfortable running, you can take the few minutes to take them on the short run up to the yard."
Cass: "Yay! I'm on it!"

We get the sheep up into the barn and all penned up ready for the work we need to do with them.

Me: "Right, back into your babies for a while now, Cass."
Cass: "Are you sure there's nothing else you need me to do? I could just lay there in the middle of the yard being a noble, loyal Border Collie."
Me: "Your puppies would probably appreciate a drink again. Back in with them you go."
Puppies: "MAMA!"
Cass: "Take me with you!"

Cass was really a very good mum overall, especially when her puppies were very small. When all eight of them started to get very mobile and lively, however, she was always more than ready to come out of the secure puppy pen for a while and come out with us for some peace and normality.

.

RENAISSANCE DOG

A beautiful fifteenth-century castle near a country village a little way from home holds a medieval festival every year. We decide one year to make the trip to check it out and take Red along with us for a day out.

Lady in ticket booth: "What a beautiful dog! Can I stroke him?"
Red: "I'm going to like this place."
Me: "Are we going to be able to fit your ego in the car on the way home?"
Red: "Shut up. I'm gorgeous. I know it. You know it. Everyone that sees me knows it."
Me: "And so modest too!"
Red: "Is it just me or are nearly all the people here dressed strangely?"
Me: "It's a medieval festival so they're wearing costumes. Look, let's go to the display ring there and see what those horses are doing."

We sit on one of the straw bales placed surrounding

the ring and watch for a few minutes before Red starts to fidget a bit.

Red: "Are we going yet?"
Me: "Not until the horses are finished, and then we can go and check out what is going on in the rest of the grounds."
Red: "Ok, I'll just sit here and look all noble. Oh, look at that man sitting on the next straw bale along. He looks lonely. If I kind of maybe bum shuffle slowly, I can probably make it over there to keep him company without you realising. Here we go…"
Man: "Excuse me, is this your dog?"

I look around to see that my traitorous Border Collie has shuffled to the very end of his lead and is pressed against the side of the man's leg, blissfully enjoying an ear scratch.

Me: "I'm so sorry. Red, come away and stop bothering the nice man."
Man: "It's fine. I like dogs and he's so well behaved."
Me: "In his own way…"
Red: "Admit it, I'm perfect."
Me: "In your own mind, maybe. The horses are done, why don't we go and have a look at some more stuff?"

We go into the next area of the festival and see a small group of people who are set up in a little area with a period style encampment set up, with longbows that they are demonstrating.

Me: "This looks interesting."
Archer: "Come try holding the bow and pulling the

string back- Oh look at your gorgeous dog! Is he ok? Does he need anything? Here, let me grab this wooden bowl and I'll go and fill it up so he can have some water."

Red: "I told you I'm going to like it here."

We continue on our way, stopping to watch the mock battle on one side of the castle. Unexpectedly a cannon goes off, startling me, and making me look round at Red, certain that he must have been scared by it. Instead, I see him looking curiously at the cannon, showing absolutely no signs of stress.

Me: "Well, that made me jump."
Red: "Wimp."

Once finished with an entire circuit of the festival showground, we decide to go and find something to eat. As I am finishing up with my drink, I feel a tug on my arm. When I look down, I see a young boy, maybe nine or ten years old.

Boy: "Can I please say hello to your dog?"
Me: "Sure you can."

I turn away for just long enough to throw my rubbish into the big bin a couple of steps away, When I turn back I see the boy kneeling down by Red, arms around his neck.

Red: "We are DEFINITELY coming back here next year."

I always called Red my grumpy old man because, at

home, he could be, particularly when it came to discussions about being groomed unnecessarily (which in Red's opinion was every time!). When out amongst people at events, he was completely and utterly in his element. I never needed to even think about stopping anyone that wanted to make a fuss of him (although would out of principle if they had not asked me if they could!)

TAKING THE DIRECT ROUTE

Finn finds the outside world very difficult to relate to on a number of ways. This is why we usually walk him early in the mornings when it is quieter. We also find methods of canine enrichment to do at home, games we can play and new tricks to learn. These give ways to exercise a dog's body and mind, to occupy them and tire them out at home if they find the world a stressful place. As Finn shows signs of being both fearful and anxious this definitely includes him, and so we find home-based entertainment while working on his confidence.

Finn: "What are you doing?"
Me: "Ah, I've got something new for us to try."
Finn: "Important question that needs answering before we begin. Will there be treats?"
Me: "Yes, there will be treats."
Finn: "Then I'm up for trying whatever it is."
Me: "It's called agility."
Finn: "What's that?"

Me: "See these pole things here? Well, some of them stick into the ground and you kind of run in between them back and forth like this."

Finn: "Well that doesn't look too difficult. You mean like this?"

Me: "That's very good. Here, have a treat. So some of the other poles sit in these little cup things on posts sticking out of the ground. This is called a jump because you jump over it."

Finn: "That makes sense."

Me: "So I'll put it on the lowest rung. You can pretty much step over it."

Finn: "Yes, yes I can. Do I still get treats for this?"

Me: "Definitely. So next we try the middle level."

Finn: "Easy. Make with the treat."

Me: "Ok, there you go. Finally, we try the highest setting. You're going to have to put a bit of effort in now."

Finn: "Too easy. What's next?"

Me: "How about we keep working on this a bit more until you've really got the idea."

Finn: "Right. Oh… What happened there?"

Me: "You knocked the pole down instead of clearing it. It's fine, you can try again."

Finn: "So you mean I don't actually have to go OVER the poles, I can go through them?"

Me: "Well, that's not really the…"

Finn: "Yeah, this is a lot easier."

Me: "Well then, how about we try going back to the middle rung."

Finn: "I can go straight through this pole as well!"

Me: "Back to the lowest level then."

Finn: "I can just step over this one."

Me: "This really isn't the idea, Finn. You're supposed

to jump over the poles and leave them still standing."
Finn: "Why?"
Me: "... I have no real answer to that question."

Technically this occurred over a couple of sessions, as it would have been too much in one go for a young dog as he was then. However many sessions we tried agility over, Finn made it very clear that he saw zero point in trying to go over when he could have just as much fun going through. A career in agility was most definitely not in his future.

A SENSE OF PURPOSE

Red was selected to come and join us to train as a working sheepdog. Previously we had bred our own dogs, but after an accident that resulted in Dillan having major leg surgery, she was spayed to avoid any risk of her getting in pup, and Cass was a little old to think about another litter from her. When Red was a few months old, we decided it was time to take him out for his first experience of working sheep alongside the experienced Dillan.

Me: "Well, Red, it's time for your big day. We're finally going to go out to the field, and you get your first chance to work sheep. Exciting, huh?"
Red: "I guess?"
Me: "So we'll go and get Dillan, and she can help you get the sheep into the barn."
Red: "Is sheep another name for a tennis ball?"
Me: "Um, no. Sheep. Big white woolly things in the field outside the farmyard? Look like little clouds walking around, eating grass?"

Red: "No, can't say I've noticed them."

Me: "Haha, you're so funny. Let's go."

Dillan: "Show me the sheep. Right now. Gotta get the sheep in. Come on, it's sheep herding time!"

Me: "Steady down, Dillan. Take a breath. It's time to start showing Red how all this works, and let him have a go at bringing them in."

Dillan: "Really? You're going to let the PUPPY do it?"

Me: "You were a puppy once, and you had to learn alongside Cass. This is exactly the same. It'll be fine."

Dillan: "Hmm."

We go into the home field where there is a flock of ewes grazing across the whole area of grass.

Me: "Ok, Red, you do what Dillan does when I give her the instructions. Exactly the same instructions as we've been introducing to you."

He lifts his head from where he is industriously investigating the hedgerow.

Red: "Whatever."

Me: "Dillan, Red, come by!"

Dillan shoots off in a big loop around the sheep to the rear, stopping on the far side of the flock and waiting for the next command. Red, on the other hand, is still at the bottom of the hedge.

Me: "Uh, Red? Come by? Off you go."

Red: "I'll pass."

Me: "This is what working sheepdogs do. It's what your parents did. It's what you're bred for. It's what we picked you out for. Come by!"

Red: "Do any of them have tennis balls? Or flying discs?"

Me: "It's a flock of sheep, of course they don't!"

Red: "That's a hard pass, thanks. If you want me, I'll be in the garden back at the house. With a tennis ball."

Me: "But... Ok, you can come out next time and try again."

Red: "There will be no next time."

He was absolutely right, there was no next time. If ever anyone needed proof that breed traits are not always guaranteed, Red was definitely proof. I have never met a less inclined dog to work sheep. The only things he ever chased in his entire life were tennis balls and discs.

TOYING WITH TIGGYWINKLE

We spent some time living and working on the farm at an agricultural college. We moved there when my husband got a job on the farm. As work was not that easy to come by at the time, and his job meant that we were living in a house on the college estate, we decided that I would go back to college for a year. (One year to take advantage of the convenience of being there and not working turned into the three-year full course because I loved it so much!) Coming from a farming background anyway, it was not long before I was fully up to date and spending college holidays working on the farm, providing cover for looking after the sheep when required. This meant spending a lot of time on the farm with the dogs.

Cass, being as fiercely independent as she was, would head off exploring the farmyard and buildings when we would take a tea break, coming back on hearing any sounds of us getting back to work. Sometimes she would bring back things she had found to play with while waiting for us.

Me: "Is that you, Cass?"

Cass: "Yeth…"

Me: "What are you doing? Why do you sound all muffled and snorty?"

Cass: "I have a new toy."

Me: "What have you found this time?"

Cass: "I told you, it's a new toy."

Me: "Huh, where did you find a spiky dog ball down here?"

Hedgehog: "What's going on? Where am I?"

Cass: "See, new toy! It has a cute little face but if I try to sniff it, this happens."

Hedgehog: "Eeek! It's going to get me!"

Cass: "And now it's a spiky toy again."

Me: "Cass… Wildlife is not for playing with!"

For anyone worrying about the hedgehog, it was absolutely unharmed by its encounter with Cass. Although it took a little while to find somewhere to release the hedgehog away from her, it wandered off into the hedgerow with no sign of injury at all. Cass was an incredibly soft-mouthed dog, especially for a breed not particularly known for being soft-mouthed. I think she was simply fascinated by this cute little creature that kept turning into a ball whenever she tried to say hello and investigate it more closely.

AN EXCITATION OF ANTICIPATION

As a young Border Collie, one thing Finn is not always blessed with is patience. When he wants to do something, it is often not easy to get him to settle down, to wait and chill out for a while. Any hint of movement can potentially lead to an explosion of excitement. Due to the fact that my husband, in particular, has a very predictable set of indicators that he is about to go and do something, some actions are always guaranteed to generate a blue merle coloured frenzy of anticipation.

Finn: "I'm bored."
Me: "Hang on a little bit longer, and then we'll do something fun."
Finn: "But why not now?"
Me: "We just need to finish sorting out what we're doing right here."
Finn: "I'll give you my squeaky parrot."
Me: "Honestly, we'll only be a few minutes more."
Finn: "Maybe the squeaky elephant?"

Me: "Not right at this second."

Finn: "Squeaky octopus it is, then. That works to get you to play every single time."

Me: "Yes, usually. But perhaps not so much when you try throwing it at my head though."

Finn: "Wait a minute, he's moving."

Me: "Relax, he's just going upstairs for a minute."

Finn: "Oh, He came back and sat down."

Me: "Soon, Finn, I promise."

Finn: "He belched. That must mean something."

Me: "Other than the fact that I married someone who can, at times, resemble some kind of revolting man pig?"

Finn: "He's got up again and gone into the kitchen."

Me: "I'm not sure. He might be nearly ready to do something."

Finn: "HE TOUCHED THE GARAGE KEYS!"

Other than Finn, I have never seen a dog that has managed to combine sneezing, jumping up, spinning in a circle and hopping on his back legs into a single kind of hybrid pirouetting movement. We can keep him somewhat calm through most things but, no matter how we have tried, touching the keys is the final straw to kick him off in excitement. The saving grace is that he does calm quickly outside, and so we have labelled the behaviour as mostly harmless.

SHOWING SOME ENTHUSIASM

At the time Red joined our group of collies at the farm, we had a flock of pedigree breeding sheep. The showing season that followed his arrival proved to be the best that we ever had, including appearances in breed championship line ups, bringing away a reserve championship and a breed championship over a couple of shows. Red was around eight months old when we took him to his first show experience. Technically dogs were not allowed in the sheep lines although, if well behaved, the other stock owners in our section had no problem with it, and a couple of us would take our dogs along rather than having to leave them at home. Until Red proved himself to be reliable and quiet around the stock lines and showing rings, we had extra people with us to keep him out of the way if necessary.

Once the showing classes finish for the day on which this takes place, we collect Red from the rest of the family and take him for his first tour of an agricultural showground.

Red: "Wow, this is all so exciting!"

Me: "I know, there's a lot going on and a lot to see."

Red: "Really exciting. Look at all the people. Sheep!"

Me: "You see sheep every day. You aren't even interested in sheep."

Red: "These are different sheep, so they're interesting. Oh, what's that?"

Me: "The big brown and white one? That's a cow."

Red: "Aha. Is that Brook over there?"

Me: "No, Brook is definitely in the field back at home. That's a different big bay horse. There are lots of horses here."

Red: "And people. Let's say hello to all the people!"

Me: "No, don't jump up. People don't like dogs who jump up at them. Keep all four paws on the floor and they'll be much happier to meet you."

Red: "But it's all so exciting!"

Me: "I know. You'll get a lot more fuss and attention if you listen to me now though."

Red: "Got it. Keep all my paws on the ground when meeting people. I can do that. Wait a minute... Skin!"

Woman: "What the hell? Did your dog just stick his nose up my skirt?"

Me: "I am so, so sorry. We're just going to go away over here where there are no people now."

Red: "What? I kept all my paws on the ground!"

He never, throughout the rest of his life, got over his obsession with finding bare human skin. We did learn from that moment on to keep his lead short when on showgrounds in warm weather.

WICKED WOOF OF THE WEST?

We live a few miles north of the south coast of England. Being located where we are we generally get a reasonable amount of rain. This being the case, it means that a lot of days see at least some rainfall in our area. Other parts of the country get as much and, in some cases, quite a bit more and so being outside in rainfall is going to happen at some point if you have dogs.

Me: "Finn, do you want to go outside?"
Finn: "Oh that sounds like a great idea. Although… maybe later?"
Me: "Are you sure? You haven't been outside for a while."
Finn: "It's fine, I don't need anything out there right now."
Me: "Ok then, back to the blanket on the sofa it is. Best way to spend a damp day."

We settle back down for a little while until Finn

starts fidgeting, sitting up and then laying back down, looking at me and whining softly. As he can do this for a number of reasons, I have to try and guess what is up with him and, given that he has not been in the garden for a while, decide to try again.

Me: "Hey, it must be time to go outside now."
Finn: "Maybe… You know what, I'm ok. Let's go back inside and maybe come outside a bit later."
Me: Well, if you're sure."

We go back inside for a little bit longer but Finn is starting to be clearly very unsettled and starting to show signs of being uncomfortable.

Me: "Right, we are going outside now. Right now."
Finn: "Honestly, I can hold it."
Me: "Finn, I can see you're arching your back and really starting to look like you're not comfortable."
Finn: "I told you, I'm fine. I don't want to go outside."
Me: "I will push you outside if I have to. You need to go outside and you need to 'go' right now."
Finn: "But look at it out there. It's raining. I HATE the rain."
Me: "Finn, you are not going to melt in the rain. You were born in Wales!"

Yes, the Welsh-born Border Collie has a pathological hatred of getting wet. He will make occasional exceptions for favourite walks or if there is a ball involved and he has not had a chance to play for a while. Other than that, apparently he WILL melt if required to step outside in the rain, no matter what I tell him.

NOT WHAT I MEANT BY DIETARY FIBRE!

I am sitting on the sofa one winter evening, watching TV and drinking a mug of hot chocolate. As always, Dillan is close by, just in case I may be in sudden and urgent need of a dog to snuggle up with or give some attention to for any reason.

Dillan: "You having anything nice, maybe some biscuits with that?"
Me: "No, no biscuits tonight. Neither you nor I really need to eat any biscuits. Or anything else like that."
Dillan: "Speak for yourself. As far as I'm concerned, it's always a good time for biscuits. If you're not going to make with anything good, I'm going to sleep."
Me: "No worries, we're not doing anything exciting tonight. You catch some sleep for a while."

All is quiet for some time, long enough to watch most of a film. I start to become aware of a weird noise, which sounds like something sort of grinding. The noise appears to be coming from almost behind me. I look over the arm of the sofa and see Dillan lying full length along the side of the sofa, head by the back corner against the living room wall. I become suspicious of what is going on - this is the 1990s and the sofa, while comfortable, has one of those fiddly, fussy trims that seem to be everywhere on the furniture of the time running along the bottom of it, with twists of rope and tassels along the whole bottom edge.

Me: "Dillan, are you chewing the sofa trim?"
Dillan: "No."
Me: "Are you sure?"
Dillan: "Definitely."
Me: "Really sure?"
Dillan: "...Yes?"
Me: "Dillan, look at me."

She turns her head towards me when I call her name again, strands of sofa trimming hanging from her mouth.

Me: "That's what I thought."
Dillan: "Next time make sure to bring biscuits."

The difficulty was in trying not to laugh, as she gave every appearance of thinking she was being covert and unnoticeable when I could clearly hear and see her every movement.

SHOOK UP BY SNOWFALL

Snow is not amazingly common where we live. If we do get some snowfall, it will usually disappear quite quickly. Occasionally, a more significant fall occurs that hangs around for a while before thawing. This happens during Finn's first winter with us. Playing in the garden with Red and us, he takes very little notice of this strange new substance. With Finn finding the world a tricky place to navigate sometimes, I decide to take the opportunity to get him out for a walk as the slippery conditions mean fewer people are likely to be out for him to be worried by.

Finn: "Is that my harness? Yay, we're going for a walk!"
Me: "We are. Now, it's a bit slippery underfoot, so let's take it nice and steady."
Finn: "Whoa, everything looks really weird!"
Me: "It's just the snow, exactly the same as in the garden at home."
Finn: "No, this is definitely different. And new. I'm not sure about new things."

We come across something that I would expect him to be spooked by, a car that has slid into the ditch at the side of the road. The driver is standing at the rear of his car and I automatically walk closer to make sure that he is ok and has managed to contact help. It is only as I turn away from the driver that I realise Finn did not react to the stranger at all. When I look at him, he is staring at the compacted snow under his paws.

Me: "Are you ok? Come on, let's get walking again."
Finn: "This stuff is weird. Where's the road? And the grass?"
Me: "It's all fine, the road and grass are still there, just under the snow."
Finn: "I suppose so. Let's walk fast, yes?"
Me: "Hold up, Finn. I don't have four legs for balance like you do. I only have two feet and it's slippery, so we need to take it steady."
Finn: "How about if I pretend to be a husky and tow you around?"
Me: "You know what? How about we take the cut-through path here across the fields? I haven't walked it before but I know where it joins with the other one."
Finn: "I know where we're going. Mush, mush!"

After a bit of a diversion when I miss a footpath sign and lose the path for a while as the snow obscures everything, we finally manage to find our way back to the end of our road.

Finn: "I can see the house. Come ON! I want to get inside and off this freaky stuff!"
Me: "Finn, I'm not a fan of skiing. We've been out in

the snow for two hours without incident, so you must be a bit calmer about it."

Finn: "Let me put it simply. What actually is snow?"

Me: "It's basically frozen water that falls in pretty shapes from the sky."

Finn. "Frozen sky water. Do you know what's another name for sky water? Rain. It's frozen bits of rain. You know I don't do rain!"

The stereotypical imagery associated with the noble dedicated Border Collie is of them looking after their charges, regardless of whatever the weather may throw at them. In many ways, it is fortunate that Finn did not join us until we had given up keeping sheep, as the flock may well have been on their own unless the weather was good!

FUNNY INTERPRETATION OF FRIENDLY

Although Red could be quirky and what I lovingly refer to as opinionated at home, when out in public he was the happiest, most tolerant dog I have personally known. He demonstrated that lovely, easy personality on a number of occasions, although one summer evening walk when we lived in the town stands out in particular.

Me: "Time to go for a walk."
Red: "Walk? Yeah, let's go, let's go! Which way are we going? Long route or short route?"
Me: "Let's go up the road and see how we feel on the way."
Red: "Onwards! So - we're at the recreation ground. It's time to make a decision. Are we going straight on for the short route, or across the rec towards the outskirts?"
Me: "Let me see... Ok, it's a nice evening. Let's cut across the rec and head for the long walk around the edge of town."

Red: "That's the right decision! Oh, those kids over there are playing football. Do you think they want a dog to join in and play?"

Me: "By play, you mean to run off with the ball, knowing you. They're not just playing, anyway. They're having a proper training session with a coach. That's the local kid's team."

Red: "So that's a no?"

Me: "That's a hard no. We're just cutting through the park to get out to the paths."

Red: "Oh well, in that case, we might as well get going."

Loose dog: "Wheeeeeee!"

Me: "Oh wow, that loose dog totally bowled over that little toy poodle!"

Red: "But he does look like he's having a really great time."

Me: "Yeah, but I'm not quite so sure about the poodle."

Red: "True. And there goes the Miniature Schnauzer as well."

Me: "Let's just keep walking. Hopefully, we can get past before he comes towards you. The last thing your arthritic hips need is being bowled over by an over-enthusiastic bigger dog, as gorgeous as he might be."

Red: "I think it might be a little late for that, he's heading this way."

Me: "Ok, you go the other side of me, on a short lead, and let's hustle towards the other side."

Man on phone: "It's ok, he's friendly."

Me: "Mine isn't!"

Red: "Hey, that's not true! I'm very friendly."

Me: "I know, it's a lie, but I really don't want you mown down by an out of control dog."

Man (still on phone): "Here boy, here boy, come here

boy."

Loose dog: "Wheeeeeee!"

Man (still on phone): "No, no, no. Come here, boy. Come here. Come HERE!"

Loose dog: "Wheeeeeee!"

Man (STILL on phone): "He's a rescue. I've only had him for two days."

Me: "… And you're letting him off in a park that in some places has open road access?"

Random man walking past: "Hey, I caught your dog."

Man (still has not even bothered to hang up the phone): "But it's ok. He's friendly!"

Me: "You might want to think about finding yourself a good dog trainer. Luckily he didn't mow down my old arthritic dog or we'd be having a 'conversation' right now."

Red: "It's all good, I'm ok. Let's just get on with our walk."

We carry on through the hedge into the other side of the recreation ground, an open space with a surfaced path, a wildlife pond and an open expanse of grass, away from the football pitches, children's playgrounds and outdoor gym equipment. We take the direct path towards the opposite gate heading to where we will hit the countryside, passing the point at which the path through the park merges with another from a side street.

Little white dog: "Grrr!"

Red: "Seriously?"

I look down to see the little white dog hanging off the hair on Red's back leg.

Owner: "Oh, look at him playing! Isn't he just so cute?"
Me: "SERIOUSLY?"

Sometimes it seemed as if Red had some kind of target showing in the merle patterning of his coat. If ever a dog minding their own business was going to get jumped on by an aggressive dog, it was him. He was never provoking. To be honest, he was never really all that interested in other dogs, even if they stole his toys while out playing. He would defend himself if he really needed to and obviously, I would get between him and trouble if I could. Somehow, even when quietly on a lead, my poor inoffensive lad had way more than his fair share. I have no idea how he stayed so sweet-tempered and tolerant with others when out.

A ROWDY RODENT

The agricultural college at which I was a student for three years had a number of parcels of land that they owned or rented for grazing livestock, dotted around the local countryside. One particular stretch of land was separated into a number of fields, just a few minutes' drive away from the main college farm. It was a very easy place to have sheep as, rather than having to haul and set up the portable sheep handling system, it actually had a permanent system set up there built out of concrete blocks. This saved a lot of time in putting up and taking down hurdles and was nicely set up to make it easy to encourage sheep to run into the pens.

Cass: "There you go. All your sheep are now in the pen."

Me: "Thanks. Go chill for a bit while we do what we need to do with them, and we can move along to the next lot."

Cass: "I'll be over there somewhere if you slow

people need them moved again."
Me: "Gee, thanks…"

A squirrel waves at her from the far side of the sheep pen. In return, Cass glares at the squirrel. Undeterred, the squirrel chitters and flicks his tail in Cass's general direction. Unable to control herself any longer, Cass jumps up on the one breeze block wide wall that runs around the outside of the sheep penning system. She runs at full speed along the top of the wall. With another flick of the tail, the squirrel disappears up the tree. Cass reaches the tree trunk, still on the top of the wall, and uses her momentum to start going up it.

Me: "Umm, Cass? Dogs don't climb trees."
Cass: "Squirrel!"
Me: "Seriously, dogs are not designed for or meant to be in trees."
Cass: "But there's a squirrel!"

She starts losing speed on her way up the way but manages to scramble onto a wide branch several feet above the ground.

Me: "So you're a tree dog now, are you?"

A black and white face peers out through some leaves.

Cass: "Uh, little help?"

One of the slow people had to go and get her out of the tree.

LESS CASANOVA, MORE CASA NO THANKS!

Most of the dogs that we have had were not spayed or neutered. Coming from farming backgrounds, there was a family history of breeding working dogs and keeping a chosen bloodline going in our working sheepdogs. The number of accidental puppies produced has been zero, as we have always been conscious of the requirements of responsible ownership, in particular when having animals that are physically capable of breeding. When it came to Red, his complete lack of interest in other dogs, even females, gave an extra level of confidence that we would not produce any unwanted puppies. Unfortunately, not everybody that has not spayed or neutered his or her dogs behaves with the same level of responsibility.

Me: "It's a lovely day. How about we sneak in a quick extra walk out to the fields?"
Red: "You know me. I'm always up for a walk."

Me: "We'll walk out through the woods to the far side and make our way back over to the bridlepath. You can run loose while we're in the fields but there might be horses on the bridlepath so I'll pop you back on the lead in case we have to move out of the way of any."

Red: "Whatever, let's get going so I can check the local canine grapevine since this morning."

We head off, enjoy a lovely relaxing walk along a woodland path, and out to the local fields with footpaths running through them that are used with the permission of the landowners. After a slow stroll around the hedgerows so that Red can indulge in a good sniff and get caught up on all the local doggy gossip, his lead goes back on and we start making our way back along the bridlepath that runs along one side of the fields and the woods.

Labrador: "Hey handsome."

Red: "Um, who are you talking to?"

Labrador: "Oh, that's such a fantastic tail you've got there."

Red: "Uh, human? What is she doing?"

Me: "I think she likes you."

Labrador: "Eaten any good poop today?"

Red: "First of all, that's disgusting. And why are you dancing around waving your butt in my face?"

Labrador: "Yeah, you know you like what you're sniffing."

Red: "Mummy, save me!"

Owner: "Oh, there you are you naughty girl! You're so playful, aren't you?"

Me: "Yeah, she's been with us for a few minutes."

Owner: "She disappeared off into the undergrowth while we were in the woods but I knew I'd find her eventually."

Labrador: "Do you like bad girls? I bet you do."

Red: "I just want to go home."

Owner: "Oh, they're so funny when they're in season, aren't they? Hahaha."

Me: "I think I should probably tell you that my dog is entire."

Owner: "Yes darling, you're having so much fun... What did you say?"

Me: My dog is entire. He's not castrated."

Owner: "WHAT? Don't you ever bother to think about how irresponsible you are to walk around with a dog that isn't neutered?"

I look at her off lead ragingly in-season bitch, who she has blithely told me disappeared from her sight for several minutes in the woods. The bitch that is currently a couple of steps removed from trying to back herself under my utterly bemused and securely on lead dog.

Me: "Yeah, lady. I'm CLEARLY the irresponsible dog owner in this situation."

Red never did cover a bitch in his entire lifetime. He never so much as reacted to being in the same place as a bitch, whether in season or not. I am not sure he ever really knew what he was supposedly biologically programmed to do in the situation.

NOT SO MUCH BROTHERLY LOVE

We get home after a very long day, having driven from just outside Brighton across England and into Wales, near Cardiff, and back again to pick up our new puppy – Finn. After unloading him from the car we give him a little while to decompress from the upset of leaving his mum and the journey, and to start investigating his new home. Once he has taken the chance to have a drink and a wee and begun exploring, I go next door to Mum's house where Red has spent the day, and fetch him home to introduce him to his new family member.

Red: "Yay, you're back. Is it time to go into the garden and play ball now?"
Me: "No, no playing ball this time. There's someone I would like you to meet."
Red: "Oh, you brought someone home to adore me in the manner that I deserve?"
Me: "Not exactly."

Red: "Someone to play ball with me and feed me lots of the treats that I like today from the little sample bag but will refuse to touch as soon as you buy a big bag of them?"

Me: "Yeah, about that... Why is it always the expensive ones you do that with?"

Red: "Because I wouldn't be me if I didn't make life complicated with food in that way."

Me: "I have to be honest, it's not one of your most endearing traits. It doesn't matter anyway. It's not someone that's here to play with you, fuss you or feed you treats."

Red: "What. Is. That?"

Me: "Red, meet Finn, your new little brother. Finn, this is Red."

Finn: "I love you."

Red: "Ugh, it's TOUCHING me. What's it doing? Make it stop!"

Finn: "We're going to be best buddies. I'm going to cuddle up to you just like this, every single night. We are going to have SO much fun. I love you."

Red: "Get it OFF me!"

Me: "Red, it's fine. He's just really pleased to meet you, He's left his family behind and now he has you. Look at him. He's small and cute and all he wants to do is cuddle up to you and go to sleep."

Finn: "I love you."

Red: "Yeah, that's definitely not happening. Ever."

Every time Finn tried to cuddle up Red shifted away. He never did anything nasty when Finn was tiny, only grumped and growled a bit at times, and we would step in and create some space. There were some arguments and fallings out as Finn got older, some of which ended with Red having a mouthful of fur. It was always Red that did the fur pulling, never Finn. For his part, Finn never stopped loving Red and never fought back. I am not entirely sure Red realised how fortunate he was, as Finn topped him by about four inches at the shoulder, and somewhere around eight or nine kilograms in weight. Finn never stopped absolutely hero-worshipping Red, utterly adoring him and deferring to him in every way possible.

OVER THE TOP

Dillan's most obvious characteristic as a working sheepdog was most definitely her enthusiasm. As an agricultural student, at times I could probably be much the same. Although not as clever and instinctively sheep savvy as her mother Cass, Dillan was much more biddable, eager to please, and obedient. Most of the time.

Farm manager: "The ewe that's been in the paddock over there for the past few days with her lambs. She's a bit lame this morning. You'll need to corner and catch her, take a look and see what's wrong with her."
Me: "No problem, I'll do that first before we go and check the sheep on the hill."
Dillan: "What? What was that? We have work to do? What work? Where? Are we going to work now? I'll help with whatever it is!"
Me: "Dillan, take a breath, for goodness' sake! It's very simple. We need to catch that ewe over there and take a look at her lame foot. She's probably just a bit

sore between her toes. We'll give all of her feet a trim, a bit of purple spray and she should be absolutely fine."

Dillan: "Ok, let's go! Time to work!"

Me: Whoa, just relax. We need to approach her slowly and quietly and then we can grab her."

College Principal: "Oh hello. I was just passing on my way over to the farm office. I'd love to watch you work."

Me: "…"

Dillan: "An audience? Even better!"

Me: "Oh for the love of… Dillan, have you suddenly lost the ability to understand any of the commands I give you?"

Dillan: "Wheeeee!"

Sheep: "To hell with all of this, I'm off."

The ewe suddenly decides that her foot is not all that sore after all and, from a standing start, pings over the stone wall surrounding the paddock as if she has springs on her feet. As Dillan, the college principal, and I all look on in shock, she starts heading for the main college campus.

Dillan: "She's getting away!"

Me: "Oh no, you're not chasing her down towards the college buildings. There are cars and access out to the roads and all sorts of things down there."

Dillan: "But, but, but…"

Me: "Into the Land Rover with you. I'll come let you out when I've got her."

After shutting Dillan in, I start jogging down towards the main campus, heading past the big greenhouses and looking down towards the main education block and workshops. A couple of horticulture students come out of the last greenhouse. They take a look at the clothes that I'm wearing and the definite hint of sheep in the air and point just back behind the greenhouse where a woolly hind end is just disappearing from view, the sheep enjoying the lush grass back there. One episode of tiptoeing and a weird sort of attempt at a rugby tackle later and I am walking the unrepentant ewe back to the farm.

Dillan: "But I would have helped!"

Dillan never did lose any of her enthusiasm for working. I really would not have changed a thing about her though, as that enthusiasm was always infectious.

THE SINGLE MINDED SHEEPDOG

We have to perform a routine husbandry task with a flock of sheep one day. We take the portable sheep penning system out to their field and set the hurdles up in a carefully selected location. The opening corridor into the pen runs alongside a fence to encourage the sheep to go inside and into the flat area, where they can be handled safely and efficiently.

Me: "Ok, Cass, time to get the girls in. Go on, get up."
Cass: "On it."

She heads out at speed around the edge of the field, gathering all of the sheep together in a single bunch. Once they are all running in the same direction and Cass is in position to steer the flock up the hill towards the pen, I call the command for her to stop and let them run straight. Cass keeps going, however, and continues turning the flock towards the other side of the field. No matter how many times I call her, she continues taking the sheep to the far corner. When she has them all contained she stops and looks back up the hill towards me.

Cass: "What are you doing up there?"
Me: "Um, let me see… I'm standing here next to the pen that the sheep are supposed to be in right now."
Cass: "The pen? Oh, you mean you want them up there in the pen? Why didn't you say anything?"

She works the flock back out of the corner without a single command from me and steers them perfectly into the pen.

Cass: "There you go. I'm off to find something disgusting to roll in and eat now."
Me: "Thanks…"

Cass had days when she was utterly convinced that she knew far better than us where the sheep should be and, in the long run, it was easier just to wait and let her get it out of her system, and then she would happily put them wherever we actually needed them to be.

Her independence working did come in very useful on the day that the sheep forced their way through the hedge into the cattle field next door when we were out. The only person around was my sister in law, who knew nothing about sheep and had come to the farm to look after her horse, and was also pregnant. She told me later that all she could think to do was take Cass out into the field where the sheep were, point towards them and ask Cass to get them back home. Cass duly complied with no hesitation and no help at all from my sister in law.

A CHIVALROUS COLLIE DOG

On a beautiful summer day, we pile into the car with Red and go on a day out to a jousting event a little way from home. We park up and unload Red, heading down to the gate to wait in line for the event to open.

Red: "This is fun. All of these people here just to adore me."
Me: "I'm not sure that's the only reason that they're all here."
Red: "Have you seen how handsome I am? Of course it is!"
Security: "Excuse me, can I say hello to your dog?"
Red: "He may."
Me: "Of course you can, he loves people."

The security guard crouches down and starts fussing Red, scratching his ears and rubbing his chest. Red keeps edging closer and closer, loving every second of it.

Security: "I should warn you that they open the day's events by letting off the cannon. A lot of dogs are scared of it."
Me: "Thanks for the warning. He's heard a cannon before and been fine with it."

At that moment the cannon goes off. Red's only reaction was to look briefly in the direction of the sound and then nudge the security person to resume fussing.

Security: "This is a seriously laid back dog! Enjoy your day."
Red: "So it's one of these medieval places again? I like these things."

We head into the ground and make our way over to where the cannon is located, as an artillery demonstration is about to begin. Despite the warning of the participants that dogs are generally terrified of the noise and run away, Red simply watches the goings-on around him. I see a little girl stop nearby, with her parents. She suddenly notices Red and ducks partly behind her mum.

Red: "Hey, what's going on? Kids love me. Why is she hiding from me?"
Me: "I don't know. Maybe she's scared of dogs."
Red: "Hmm."

We continue watching the demonstration and, other than ensuring I have got hold of his lead and he is close enough to me not to get in anyone else's way, I let him lay quietly next to my feet while I am watching what's occurring behind the ropes. A couple of minutes later I feel him starting to move around and look down to see him shifting about and glancing at the girl.

Red: "I don't get it. Why would anyone be scared of me?"
Me: "I don't know. Just stay there quietly for now, ok?"

He keeps glancing at her and shifts so he is lying on his side to be a little bit closer. Then he starts rolling and scratching his back in the grass, sneezing to get attention. When that does not work, he brings his front legs up to rub at his eyes, repeatedly stopping to peek around a leg so that he can check whether the little girl is watching or not. She is and shifts back around her mum a little closer to him.

Seeing that she has moved, Red sits back up beside me. Out of the corner of my eye, I can see her edging closer. I am normally very strict about people asking before approaching my dog but I can see Red is totally fine with her getting closer and has been pulling out all his best cute to make it happen, so on this occasion, I let it go. Gradually she moves closer and closer, finally touching his ear with a single fingertip before heading back to mum again.

Red: "My work here is done. Let's go and find more people to adore me."

Later in the day, we find the main ring and settle down in preparation to watch the jousting. Red appears to be contentedly snoozing in the grass, so I put the loop of the lead securely around my wrist and leave him to sleep in peace. A while later I can hear giggling behind me and realise that the lead is now taut at its full length.

Me: "Red, what are you doing?"
Red: "Nothing!"

I look back and see two kids, with their separate families, that we had met earlier in the day, with a very familiar blue merle collie wriggling back and forth between them, merrily sharing their food and ice cream.

Me: "Nothing, huh?"
Red: "I can't help it if everyone I meet loves me!"

DIFFERENT KIND OF FOOD RUN

As sadly happens as dogs get older, Roo began to slow down with age. Although the brain still very much wanted to go, the body simply could not cope with as much physical exercise as when she was a younger dog. This meant we needed to try to find creative ways to exercise body and mind and have some fun with her. What turned out to be her favourite game of all was discovered by accident.

Me: "Hey Roo, I bought these really nice little treats for Finn but he doesn't like them very much. Would you like to try some?"
Roo: "It's food. Is grass green?"
Me: "I didn't think there was a lot of risk, to be honest."
Roo: "What's that supposed to mean?"
Me: "I just know you really like your food. So what do you think?"
Roo: "I'm not sure. Give me another one to try."
Me: "There you go."

Roo: "Yeah, I can definitely take these off Finn's paws."

Me: "Great, better than they're appreciated. Here, have another one. Oh whoops, I dropped it. It's gone skidding off over the floor."

Roo: "On it. Wheeeee!"

Me: "Phew, I thought it was going to go under the fridge."

Roo: "Again!"

Me: "I'm sorry?"

Roo: "Throw another one!"

Me: "You want me to throw the treats on to the floor?"

Roo: "Yes! Throw them along the floor so I can chase them and pounce on them."

Me: "Ok, if you insist."

Roo: "Wheeeee!"

And so Roo's favourite game in her later years was born: take five or six little bone-shaped treats, throwing them one by one across the laminate kitchen floor so that they slid well. Roo would jump and skip after them, slapping at them with her front paws to try and stop them, and then come prancing back, smiling with excitement in anticipation of the next treat being launched.

A BOUNDLESS BALL OF ENTHUSIASM

Finn can be very enthusiastic about life in general, as you might expect from a young Border Collie. Some things prompt even higher enthusiasm than others.

Finn: "La la la, this is nice. There's no one around as it's really early, it's a lovely fresh summer morning and I've really got the hang of this loose lead walking thing now. Oh… I see you brought the ball chucker this morning. We must get to the park immediately."
Me: "It's ok, Finn. It's a ten- to twelve-minute walk to get to the park, so you'll be all nice and warmed up by the time we get there and you start running after the ball a few times."
Finn: "I bet we can make it there in seven…"

Approximately eight minutes later, we emerge into the local park, one of us a little breathless. The other party is now bouncing sideways, although always carefully within the loose lead boundaries, and squeaking a bit, eyes on stalks at anything in view.

Finn: "Ducks! Let's chase the ducks!"
Me: "Leave them alone. We're going to the other side of the park and we'll play ball for a few throws."
Finn: "Magpies! Let's chase the magpies!"
Me: "Leave them alone, we're going to go to the other side of the park and play ball."
Finn: "Seagulls! Let's chase the seagulls!"
Me: Starting to feel a bit like a skipping record. "Leave them alone, we're going to go to the other side of the park and play ball."
Finn: "Ok, we're at the other side of the park now. Oh… The lead is coming off… YAY BALL!"

A few minutes and half a dozen throws of the ball later:

Me: "Right, time to carry on with our walk."
Finn: "One more."
Me: "No, we're carrying on."
Finn: "ONE. MORE."
Me: "Nope, I'm going to put your lead on so that we can walk along this little bit of road, and then you can go off lead for a good run while we make our way across the fields."
Finn: "I'm going to bounce on the lead and stare at the ball chucker. Oh, we're walking. Seagulls!"
Me: "Leave them alone, we're going to the fields."
Finn: "Oh, ok. CAT!"
Me: "It's just staring at you, nothing more. It's fine."
Finn: "But, but, but… Cat! Oh wait, here's the bridge over the stream into the fields. Horse poo!"
Me: "Do NOT eat the horse poo."
Finn: "Oh, ok. Treat?"

Me: "Finn, you're free. Go, run around and do dog stuff."
Finn: "Horse poo!"
Me: "OTHER dog stuff, that isn't eating horse poo!"
Finn: "Oh, ok. Treat?"

A little while later we reach the other side of the fields, about to head back along a public road.

Me: "That's it, Finn. Time to go back on the lead and start heading home for breakfast."
Finn: "Treat? Right, onwards to breakfast!"
Me: "Wait up. Remember the whole loose lead thing."
Finn: "Onwards, full speed ahead!"
Me: "Slow down a bit! I don't walk that fast."
Finn: "Onward… Ok, I suppose I can slow down. I'll be good and walk next to you. Treat?"

DUCKING THE ISSUE

We are lucky enough to live near a beautiful area of open forest. Not the kind of forest with trees, but an ancient hunting ground from the Norman times following the Conquest and the Battle of Hastings in 1066. It is now the largest public access space in the south-east of England and is crisscrossed with paths and tracks. This is somewhere that we took Red to on a number of occasions and then when he was old enough for the longer walks, we began to take Finn as well.

Me: "Here we go boys, out you get. We're on the Forest. Once we're away from the road a little further you can go off lead and have a run."
Red: "Onwards."
Finn: "Red, Red, look at me! Look at me, Red. I'm playing over here. Come and play with me!"
Red: "Did we really have to bring him?"
Me: "Be nice. He utterly hero worships you, even if you are a cranky old man to him."

Finn: "Come on, Red. Let's run! Come ON!"

Red: "We could leave him here, seeing as he likes it so very much?"

Me: "We are not leaving Finn on the Forest just because you're having a grump. Come on, which way are we going?"

Red: "This way, so we can go along the big ridge."

Finn: "Yay, let's run!"

Me: "Ok Finn, calm down. Don't go too far, or get out of sight."

Red: "Come on, I want to go to the pond."

Me: "This way, Finn. Just follow Red, he knows the way."

Red: "That's it, Finn. Keep following me. This way. Let's go into the pond for a drink."

Finn: "Oh, I'm not so sure about the water."

Red: "It's fine, keep coming this way."

Finn: "I'm a little bit scared now."

Me: "Uh, guys?"

Red: "This way. It'll be fine."

Finn: "I can't feel the bottom."

Me: "Really, guys?"

Red: "I don't know what your problem is, I'm standing here just fine."

Me: "Uh oh. Finn, come back this way."

Finn: "Argh! I can't feel the bottom. Must keep trying to run."

Me: "No! Finn, come back this way. You're going deeper!"

Red: "Keep going, kid. Trying jumping to get further through the water. You're doing fine."

Me: "Are we going to have to come in and get you? Yes! Turn back this way. That's it, keep coming back this way."

Finn: "Scared!"

Me: "Ok, just a little bit more. There you go, you're out and safe now."

Red: "Huh. Whatever. Can we get on with our walk now?"

Me: "Um, Red? Did you just try to drown Finn?"

Red: "No comment?"

I am still not sure what caused Finn to start leaping deeper into the pond, but we seriously thought we were going to have to wade in after him, which was not a pleasant thought as this took place in cold weather. It took quite some time before we could persuade Finn to step in a puddle, and rather a lot longer before he would again try entering a pond.

SNOW QUEEN

Although our dogs very firmly live in the house with us now, there have been times when our working dogs lived outside. It is not the way we would choose for them to live now, but that was the situation back when this story took place. Their living conditions were carefully worked out, however, with comfortable beds inside enclosed wind and rainproof shelters, and with outside space they had permanent access to and could use at will twenty-four hours a day.

Me: "Wow, it really snowed overnight. That's got to be five or six inches deep out there, if not more. I bet I'm going to have a hard time persuading the dogs to get out of bed this morning."
Dillan: "Yeah, I looked out of my kennel door earlier and went back to bed. I mean, I guess I COULD come out if we have really important work to do. Or if you have really good treats or something."
Me: "No, you stay in your nice warm bed. All the ewes are in the barn, and we'll get out to check the

rams and tegs* later. I'm just going to check on Cass and then leave you guys in peace."

Dillan: "A snack would be nice?"

Me: "Come on Cass, rise and shine. Cass? Where are you, girl?"

By this point, almost the entire upper half of my body is squeezed through the door of the other shelter, and there is no sign of Cass inside.

Me: "Cass? Where on earth are you?"

Suddenly the snow next to my leg starts to move a little and then seems to erupt, snow spraying absolutely everywhere as it is rapidly thrown from the emerging form of a shaking Border Collie.

Cass: "What? Anyone would think it's supposed to be cold!"

Cass would almost always choose to sleep outside given the choice. Her only exception was for very heavy rain with high winds as she would get wet and chilled. Any other weather conditions were fair game to sleep outside.

*Tegs: yearling sheep, the lambs born the previous year that are being reared on to be the breeding stock in the future.

CENTRE OF (IN)ATTENTION

Red definitely enjoyed having days out and was the kind of dog we could take anywhere. With his very eye-catching blue merle markings, he would get plenty of attention and loved every second of it. On this one particular day, we have taken him to a sort of motorbike gathering with stalls selling all kinds of bike-related things, at the local county showground. There are a few other dogs there but not many, and Red seems to be thoroughly enjoying himself wandering around sniffing and checking out everyone passing by in case they might feel a sudden and urgent need to fuss a dog.

Me: "We're just going to wait here while he goes into this building. Dogs aren't allowed, I'm afraid."
Red: "Huh, I'm tidier and better behaved than most people."
Me: "Yeah, you know that and I know that. But rules are rules, so we shall stand over here in the shade while we wait for him."

Red: "I shall soak up some adoration while we wait."
Me: "Adoration? From who?"
Red: "You know how it goes when we're out anywhere. People see me, then they ask you if they can say hello or fuss me, and then the adoration begins."
Me: "I'm not sure there will be quite so much adoration from the middle-aged bike crowd here as you're used to."
Red: "Have you seen how gorgeous I am?"
Me: "Oh trust me, I know. I just don't want you to be disappointed."

We stand there and wait. Red puts on his very best noble, faithful dog impression, tail waving gently whenever anyone comes out of the door. One by one, they walk past him, paying him absolutely no attention at all. His tail drops every time and then lifts again when the next person comes out, only to have the procedure repeated. By the time my husband emerges, I am feeling sad for my beautiful loving boy, and have lost my enjoyment of the day. We decide to start making our way towards the exit, via the parking area when some bikes are parked up on display.

Woman: "Hi. Could I and my little boy say hello to your dog?"
Me: "Sure, go right ahead. He loves people."
Red: "And normality is restored. Bring on the adoration!"

CONNIVING COWS

Among the things that Finn is less than keen on are other animals. Cats are his real nemesis and require immediate scaring off as soon as he sees them (as long as they do not stand up to him, in which case they no longer exist and are completely ignored). Sheep used to be scary but now provoke little more than a bit of huffing if they appear in a place they were not last time he went that way. Cows are rather more of an issue as far as he is concerned.

Me: "Through this gate onto the footpath through the farm fields then."
Finn: "Wait a minute, what are those things ahead of us?"
Me: "Those are cows. There aren't any with calves though so if we walk nice and quietly through here, we should be absolutely fine."
Finn: "They look dangerous."
Me: "Relax, it will be fine. They shouldn't bother us."

Finn: "I'd better tell them to leave us alone, just in case. Oi, you! Don't you come near us or… I'll bite your nose! I'm big and noisy and I'm definitely not scared of you at all so you'd better keep away from us!"

Cow: "Keep your fur on, pal. We're just eating grass here."

Finn: "Yeah well, it had better stay that way. Or else."

Cow: "Yeesh, take a breath. We'll all move over this way a bit, ok?"

Me: "Leave them be, Finn. See? They've all moved off the path now so we have a clear route right over to the gate out of this field."

Finn: "Well… I guess it's ok."

Me: "There you go, we're past all of the cows now, and nearly out of the field."

Finn: "Hang on. If we're past them all that means they're all behind us. Emergency, emergency! The cows are chasing us!"

Me: "They are doing no such thing! They've merely moved back onto where the footpath runs once we've passed so that they can eat the grass there."

Finn: "No, they're behind us so therefore they must be chasing us. I'll just keep turning around and giving them my very best mean glare to make sure they stay away from us."

Me: "They are mostly facing the other way. We'll be away from them faster if we just get on with it!"

Finn: "No, these cows are sneaky. They're planning something, I'm sure of it!"

He had to have a final grumble at the (totally disinterested) cows once we had gone through the gate into the next field and shut it behind us.

Apparently, anyone or anything behind Finn is up to no good and requires close watching, although cows do not seem to be plotting against him so much any more according to his behaviour walking through the fields now.

THE TREATMENT HE DESERVES

While fulfilling the role of lorry dog at the company for which my husband drives, Red became kind of adopted by everyone there, being treated as the 'company dog'. This involved having his own water bowl, labelled with his name, MANY tennis balls stashed around the place and probably far more than his share of the regular junk food fest known as 'Fat Friday'. Red's perspective on his working life seemed to position things a little differently. As far as he was concerned, he was not the company dog. In his mind, he was the boss, and everyone else there was his staff. This became obvious one day when my husband asked me to drop something into work for him.

Me: "Hey Red."
Red: "Oh, hi. What are you doing here?"
Me: "Running some errands as requested. What about you?"
Red: "Oh you know, the usual. Supervising things here, playing ball, keeping all of my minions in line."

Me: "Your what?"

Red: "My minions. You know what I mean, my staff. I have to keep them in line. Keep refreshing their training, so that they know exactly what's expected of them."

Me: "That's… kind of cynical. You mean you think that you're in charge of all the guys here?"

Red: "Yep."

Me: "I'm sure that's not really the case. You just think you're in charge."

Red: "Huh, watch this."

He trots over to a pile of metal rods that are stacked up in the yard. There is a tennis ball clearly in sight behind the first row of metal. He could easily reach it by ducking under the (safely and securely stacked) metal and stretching his neck a little. Instead, he starts barking.

Red: "Minions! Minions!"

Worker: "Hey, what's up boy?"

Red: "Minion, fetch my ball."

Worker: "Aw, can't you reach your ball? Here you go."

Red: "Now throw it."

Worker: "Here, I'll throw it for you."

Red: "I don't feel like going and fetching it right now. You go."

Worker: "There you are, one ball all safe and sound."

Red: "Now throw it."

After a little while longer the worker disappears back off to whatever he was doing in the workshop, leaving me outside in the yard with Red.

Red: "You see?"

Me: "Wow."

Red: "At least there is one place I get the proper treatment I deserve."

He really had just about the entire company trained as he wanted them, Even the boss would come out for a quick game of football if he thought nobody was looking, and Red was always happy to oblige.

HOARDER COLLIE

This anecdote comes from events that happened more years ago than I really want to contemplate now, from a time before the prevalence of pet theft that there is now. In more recent times I would never leave a dog completely unsupervised in a garden because the risk these days is just too high. These events also took place in a little group of houses down a very quiet, private dead-end lane on a working farm, where everyone was used to watching out for loose livestock and drove with according care. Again, I would not do this now, as where we live the roads are busier and there is no livestock here to create that caution!

Me: "Cass, we're going out for a while. It's a lovely day so you can stay in the garden. There's a big bowl of fresh water in the shed there, and you can go in there if it does happen to rain, or under the apple tree for shade. Be good, stay here, and we'll be back in a little while."

Cass: "Got it. I'll be right here when you get back."

A little while later, we returned home. The garden gate is still firmly closed, the dog is basking in the sun on the grass, and there is no indication that anything of any great interest has happened.

Me: "Hey Cass. Were you a good girl?"

She kicks something out of sight in the shed.

Cass: "Oh yes, definitely."
Me: "Wait a minute, what have you got there?"
Cass: "Nothing… Why don't we go inside? It must be nearly time to feed me again or something."
Me: "Well, if you're sure you've been good. Let's go and find some dinner."

We move to later that week when I answer a knock at the door and find a neighbour standing outside.

Neighbour: "Hi. This is a bit awkward but can I have my dog toys back?"
Me: "Excuse me?"
Neighbour: "My dog's toys. Your dog took them."
Me: "Cass? I don't think she did. We left her here when we went out the other day, but she was safely contained in the garden while we were gone, just like she always is if we go out and leave her at home."
Neighbour: "Would you mind just having a quick look to see?"
Me: "Of course, although I don't expect to find anything."

We go out into the garden where there are no toys that I do not recognise, so we move into the shed. Tucked into a hidden corner, out of obvious sight, is a pile of strange dog toys. I send the neighbour on their way with many apologies and their poor dog's toys.

Me: "Cass, did you get out of the garden and steal toys from the other dogs in the houses while we were gone?"
Cass: "Would you believe me if I said no?"

It turned out that she was wriggling through a tiny hole in the back hedge and getting into the garden of the house backing onto ours. She had been doing this for some time, but somehow she always managed to be safely back in our garden waiting for us when we got home, and this was the first we'd heard of it. Safe to say, it never happened again, and if we went out, Cass was very definitely confined to the house.

PAVEMENTS ARE FOR DOGS!

We have been fortunate to have lived most of our lives in rural surroundings. Even in the few years that we spent living in a local town, ten minutes brisk walking brought us along a few roads to a network of paths that circled the outskirts of the town. With relatively little effort, we could find ourselves in the middle of a beautiful green space. Red and I spent many very happy hours wandering in these fields and paths as part of our daily routine. Some of the routes on the way to pick up the path involved roads with full pavements both sides, while a few stretches ran along country lanes, bordered by hedges close to the tarmac or extremely narrow verges.

Red: "We're going for a nice walk, yes?"
Me: "We are. We're just going to walk along the pavement here, then there's a short stretch of the narrow lane. You can hop up on that soft little verge if you want."

Red: "No, that's fine. It's really narrow and I can just trot along here either right next to you or just in front."

Me: "Are you sure? The verge will be a lot softer on your paws."

Red: "No, I'm tough. I'll trot along the road."

Me: "Well, if you're sure. You can run all over the grass in the fields soon."

Red: "There's a path there too, isn't there?"

Me: "Yes…"

Red: "I do like a nice path."

After a few years in town, we move back to the same rural village where we had previously lived on the farm. A couple of short stretches of road have pavements running on both sides. Quite a bit of the village has single pavements on one side only, and a number of lanes wend around the outskirts, mostly with grass verges, or narrow pavements with a strip of grass running alongside. This road setup leads to a few discussions on how a canine and human pairing should walk on some of these routes.

Me: "Ok Red, the pavement is narrow and there's someone coming the other way. Why don't you just hop up on that verge while they go past us?"

Red: "Don't want to."

Me: "Seriously? Just for a second. Never mind then, I'll just squeeze behind you while we pass."

Red: "That's a much better idea."

Me: "And now we're leaving the pavement behind. Let's walk through the grass and avoid all the loose, possibly sharp stones on the edge of the road."

Red: "Let's not."

The walk continues on in this vein, with Red only deigning to remove paws from tarmac surfaces when in fields or woods, on footpaths or bridlepaths with no other option. As we are making our way back towards home, we again reach a stretch with a very narrow strip of verge. I notice a car in the distance travelling towards us. This is a very narrow country road, and I really want Red to be up on the verge when the car passes so that I can be between him and the car to be sure that the car will not miss the fact that he is there and hit him.

Me: "Red, shift up onto the verge for me."
Red: "Nope."
Me: "There's a car coming. Move over onto the verge and give me room to stand next to you."
Red: "Pavement is for dogs!"

We never could shake his opinion on the fact that tarmac surfaces and pavements existed for him to walk on, and learned that we just had to walk around him if necessary. On a few occasions, I ended up having to push him gently onto verges with my knees and hold him there with my body while the vehicle passed, which would result in some very dirty looks from him. Fortunately, he had zero chase drive, and would happily walk along the pavement or side of the road on lead perfectly no matter what was going on around him unless asked to put a paw on dirt or grass when the pavement was available. Pavements, as far as Red was concerned, were definitely for dogs.

ABANDONED IN COMPANY

Given the choice, Finn remains utterly convinced that his humans require canine supervision most of the time. He can cope with the two of us being in different places so long as he knows where we are, and he is with one of us. He is often less than happy if one of us is inside the house and the other outside, as he believes that this means he is missing potential playtime. He is fine when my husband heads off to work early in the morning as this fits his routine. If he goes out later in the day, however, as sometimes happens if he has errands to run at the weekends, Finn does not take it quite so well.

Finn: "Where's he going?"
Me: "He has to go into town. He won't be very long."
Finn: "He went without us?"
Me: "Well yes, there's no point in going with him as he's only going to be gone for a little while."
Finn: "He left us behind?"

Me: "He's going to be out for an hour, at the absolute maximum."

Finn: "But he went without us!"

Me: "Finn, relax, He will be back before you know it."

Finn: "What if he isn't?"

Me: "He will be."

Finn: "But what if he isn't? What if he never comes back?"

Me: "Finn, I guarantee he will be coming back."

Finn: "No, he's gone. He left us. We're never going to see him again. He ran away and left me here with just you."

Me: "Gee, thanks. That's flattering. Way to make me feel loved."

Finn: "Is he back yet?"

Me: "It's been five minutes, at most. Not yet."

Finn: "What about now?"

Me: "Six minutes."

Finn: "What about NOW?"

Me: Six and a half minutes."

Finn: "HE'S NEVER COMING BACK! HE'S ABANDONED US!"

About half an hour later, we hear the car pulling up outside.

Finn: "Who's that? Wait a minute… Is that his car out there?"

Me: "You know exactly what his car sounds like."

Finn: "Is it? Did he? Oh, hurry up, hurry UP!"

His tail starts to wag as he hears the gate open and close, and a key in the door. By the time the door opens, Finn is pretty much tap dancing.

Finn: "I thought you were never coming home! You were gone FOREVER!"

No matter how many times this has happened, one of us going out and leaving him at home with the other means that we have abandoned him and are never coming back!

BIG IS BETTER!

Red was one of the most mannerly dogs I have had. Beautifully considerate of most personal space, his worst habit was what happened on finding that someone he wanted to throw the ball for him was paying him no attention. He would circle around behind them and they would suddenly sprout a blue merle coloured nose from between their knees, which would then retreat, leaving a tennis ball wedged between them. On the list of things he most definitely did not do were whining to get something he wanted unless feeling ill, or jumping up at people.

This story occurs one day in summer, somewhere between the tennis at Wimbledon and the beginning of the school summer holidays. While shopping in my local supermarket, I spot a display of tennis equipment. On one of the shelves are a number of huge tennis balls. As Red always enjoys playing with tennis balls, I decide to get him one and take it back to where he has spent the morning with Mum so far.

Me: "Mum, look at this."

Mum: "Oh boy, he's going to love that!"

Me: "Red, come here please."

Red: "I'm coming, I'm coming. Keep your hair… Is that what I think it is?"

Me: "Well, that depends on what you think it is. If you think it's the largest tennis ball that you've ever seen, then you would be right."

Red: "It's huge. And so round. And so ball-like. Whose is it?"

Me: "I'm not sure. Do we know anyone that likes tennis balls? Maybe somebody sort of shaped like a dog? And a spotty kind of grey, black, ginger and white coloured?"

Red: "Not really… Wait a minute – that sounds a bit like me. Is it mine?"

At this point, my exceedingly polite and well-mannered dog starts flinging himself into the air or directly up at me, almost crying in pure excitement as I am taking the net wrapping off the ball. I throw it across the floor and watch the joyous scramble of legs flying in all directions as Red takes off after it.

Red: "Wheeeee!"

The novelty of his giant tennis ball never did wear off. It even survived until the following year, when it also became one of the favourite toys for Finn for a while, even though when first introduced to it, tennis ball and puppy were approximately the same size. The giant ball died of natural causes when the rubber perished and the air leaked out. I still keep an eye out if I go to the supermarket but have yet to see another one there. (A friend of mine proofread the first draft of this book and brought Finn his own giant tennis ball as a gift when she came to visit, so he now has one of his own.)

CPS - COLLIE POSITIONING SYSTEM

One of the greatest things about living and working in the countryside is the fantastic places in which you get to spend your days. Working on the land or having your own holding means access to more than the public paths, frequently during the working day. One task undertaken on some farms that grow crops is one called rogueing. This involves walking through a growing crop and pulling the rogue weeds, the unwanted plants growing amongst the crop, out by hand. This cuts down on the amount of chemical pesticide that needs to be applied and the number of vehicles that have to travel over the land. While I am walking through the crop pulling the rogues, Cass is running free in the field. She is having a wonderful time doing dog things. Following her nose, scaring out some bunnies and running along the tramlines, the wheel marks left through the crop for the machinery to follow.

Me: "Cass, don't go too far. Stay in this field."

A black and white head pops up over the ears of the crop.

Cass: "Where are you?"
Me: "Over here, right where I was just now."
Cass: "Oh, ok."

She disappears for a few minutes before popping up again.

Cass: "Where are you?"
Me: "I'm over here. Just a little bit along from where I was last time.
Cass: "Ok."

She vanishes again for a little bit longer before coming close enough for me to see her through the growing crop, although with her back to me so not realising how close she is. I watch as she rears up into her back legs and starts bouncing along like some kind of weird black and white wallaby.

Cass: "Where are you? Where are you? WHERE ARE YOU?"

The longer she is looking, the more she bounces along on her back legs prolonging the wallaby comparison. It is all I can do not to chuckle.

Me: "Easy, Cass. I'm over here."
Cass: "Phew. I mean… Are you laughing at me?"
Me: "Who, me? Never!"

QUIRKY CANINE

Red was not typically what could be called possessive. He could grump a bit if you got too close when he was eating his food, so we would leave him in peace after putting the food down, but he never really bothered much about other things. There were, however, two notable exceptions: his lorry at work, and his car.

Me: "Let's load up, Red. We're all going for a ride."
Red: "Always up for a ride, you know that. Who is this 'all' you mention?"
Me: "You, the both of us, and…"
Red: "Wait, is that Nan? In my car?"
Me: "Yes, Nan is coming with us. You know you love her."
Red: "Well yes, but in my car?"
Me: "You're not that big, you don't need the whole of the back seat. Be nice, we could just leave you at home instead."
Red: "Ok. I suppose."

We go on our way for a while and have to stop for a bathroom break at a supermarket. Nan (my mum) and I head into the store and back out as quickly as we can. As Mum opens the door to get back into the back seat, the doorway is filled by a large amount of indignant blue merle fluff.

Red: "You're not getting into MY car. Back off!"
Mum: "Wow, he's never been quite like that before."
Me: "Yeah, he'll push people around in what he regards as his vehicles if he can get away with it."
Red: "It's my car!"
Me: "Stop being ridiculous and let Nan in the car."
Red: "If I have to."
Me: "You have remembered who carries the biscuits?"

He subsides with some small amount of grace and moves back to leave room for Mum to get back into the car and we carry on again for a while.

Mum: "Um, I'm not really very happy back here."
Red: "My car, you shouldn't be in here."
Me: "Is he really bad?"
Red: "MY car!"
Me: "Right, we're pulling over the very next chance that we get."

Just a few minutes later, we pull into a layby. My very relieved Mum gets out of the back to swap seats with me.

Red: "I won, I won. I get the whole back seat now. Oh, it's you. Have I told you recently how much I love you? Here, let me cuddle up on your lap and sleep for the whole rest of the journey."

This was one of his quirks but it was only on this one trip that he ever behaved quite this extremely with Mum in the car. The extent of his protests when she came out with us was usually barking on trying to get back in. I can only put the abnormally grumpy behaviour with her on that day down to not feeling quite right. Red did at other times demonstrate an ability to push people around if he thought he could scare them and get his own way. Nan was not normally on his list of victims! (Yes, he understood who was meant by the name Nan. He knew Mum, Dad and Nan to know who we were referring to.)

GARDEN WARFARE

Roo was the sweetest little dog, who loved just about everyone and everything. She had two exceptions: rats and squirrels. When she first came to live with my mum and sister, the house backed onto open fields, which meant that frequently quite a bit of wildlife visited the garden. This was increased (and still is to this day) by the fact that Mum enjoys watching wild birds in the garden and so puts food out for them.

Me: "Right, that's all the bird feeders filled up out there. That should keep them happy for a while."
Squirrel: "Guys? Hey, guys? They've put fresh food out. There are wild bird seed and suet balls. And - oh yes, they have put out fresh peanuts. Squirrel party time!"
Roo: "I think I heard something."
Me: "It's probably birds. They like it when the feeders are all full."
Roo: "No, I'm not sure it was birds. It sounded a lot more... furry."

Squirrel: "This way, kids. Over there to the peanut feeder. Fill your faces."
Roo: "Definitely furry. I need to be outside."
Me: "Hang on a minute and I'll let you out when we've put all off the bird feeding stuff away again."
Squirrel: "Hah, the little shouty white one is stuck inside! Nah Nah! What are you going to do about it, shouty little white dog?"
Roo: "Come on, let me out, met me out!"
Me: "Ok, that's everything put away. Here you go, Roo. Let's open the door so you can go outside if you want."
Roo: "RAAAAAH!"
Squirrels: "Scatter!"

For a few seconds, it seemed like I could hear squirrel claws scrabbling in all directions as they scattered over the roofs of the garden sheds, making for the safety of the trees. What they never realised (and I am not too sure Roo ever really thought about it either) is that they were perfectly safe as she had no hope of reaching them once they were off the ground.

PRACTICAL PRIORITIES

In many ways, Red was not a typical dog. He rolled in only two substances: freshly mowed grass and snow. He absolutely hated any kind of mess and had a pathological hatred of being dirty. If he did come in wet and muddy after a walk, he would disappear into his bed and emerge thirty minutes later, spotlessly clean and gloriously fluffy coated. Certain circumstances could, however, override his normal inclination and make him forget his loathing of the wet stuff.

Red: "Hey, will you throw the ball?"
Me: "I'm busy here, Red."
Red: "Ah, come on and throw the ball."
Me: "It's stopped raining for the first time in days, so I want to get the herb garden straightened out."
Red: "Please just throw the ball. I'm only going to keep shoving it at you or throwing it at you until you give in and throw it."
Me: "Ok, ok! Here you go. I threw the ball."

Red: "Again!"

Me: "You're not going to give in, are you?"

Red: "You know me so well."

Me: "Wait a minute, what are you doing?"

Red: "What do you mean?"

Me: "Why are you running around like that?"

Red: "Like what? I'm simply fetching the ball back."

Me: "You're charging over the wet, muddy bit of garden after the ball, right?"

Red: "Yeah, what of it?"

Me: "But once you've picked the ball up, you tiptoe your way round to the path and do your very best twinkle toes trot along that to get back."

Red: "Well yeah, you know I don't do getting dirty."

Me: But you're charging straight through the mud after the ball, so you're already dirty before you get near the path."

Red: "Well, obviously. It's a tennis ball, it's important!"

No, it made no sense to me either. Mud collected while actively chasing a just thrown or kicked ball apparently did not count.

SWELTERING SUMMER SNUGGLES

At the age of eight months, Finn made it very clear to anybody within earshot that he did not enjoy being shut in his crate overnight. After a quick check over of the bedroom to make sure that it was puppy safe and that he could not get to anything I would be upset to lose if he chewed it, I tried letting him out of the crate. He immediately hopped up onto the bed and settled down with a hugely contented sigh. He never made a mess or damaged anything once given the run of the room overnight. It was not until we hit a stretch of very hot weather that he demonstrated his most irritating night-time habit.

Me: "Ok Finn, time for bed."
Finn: "Wow, it's hot up here."
Me: "Oh yes, it's toasty everywhere. We have all of the upstairs windows open, but there's still not a hint of a breeze. All we can do is try and get through the night as cool as possible."
Finn: "You try being me with a big fur coat on."

Me: "You've got two different flat beds on the floor, your crate is open with another bed in there, and my bed. Or you can sleep anywhere on the floor. Pick the coolest spot you can find."

He shifts from spot to spot around the room, eventually settling on the carpet underneath the open window while I am reading the next chapter of my book. I finish the chapter, closing the book and putting it down. Before I can move to turn out the bedside light, Finn hops up onto the bed and snuggles into my side.

Me: "What on earth are you doing?"
Finn: "It's time to go to sleep. That means it's time to cuddle up."
Me: "This room is around the same temperature as the surface of Mercury, and you want to cuddle up?"
Finn: "I think there might be a bit of an exaggeration in that statement?"
Me: "Ok, so that is physically impossible, but it's still way too hot for snuggling. We'll never get to sleep."
Finn: "Zzzzz."

I mentioned this to a friend, whose response was that I would very much appreciate the furry hot water bottle when winter came around. Fast forward a few months:

Me: "Brr! The heating's gone off for the night. Time to go and get comfy under the covers."
Finn: "Race you up the stairs!"

Me: "Ok, I'm settled under here, and the covers are all straight so you can jump up here for the bedtime snuggle."

Finn: "No, I'm good."

Me: "Really? It's cold in here! You don't want to be on the nice warm bed?"

Finn: "Ok, if you insist."

Me: "That's it, come and cuddle up for the night... Wait, where are you going?"

Finn: "Oh, I'm just going to curl up down here."

Me: "Seriously? You're all over me when it's ridiculously hot, but right down at the foot of the bed when it's cold? Are you for real?"

Finn: "Zzzzz."

No, I still cannot understand how that works! The summer we are in the middle of as I write this has again produced a heatwave, and again I had a dog glued to my side on the hot nights. Now it has cooled down a little again, he has decamped to sleep on a different bed.

PURLOINED BY A PUPPY

Frequently Red managed to give us the impressions that he just did not understand other dogs. He would happily say hello to any dog that wanted to interact, ignore any that did not appear to want to be sociable and often stared in a bemused fashion at dogs partaking in a 'rough and tumble' where he could see them. In many ways, he never really seemed to think of himself as being a dog.

At one point on the circular route around the town in which we lived was a series of two or three little paddocks, all interconnected. This was where many of the local dogs and their owners came to play. Red and I were no exception, as Red would regularly bring me there to play ball. He knew exactly where in the walk these fields were and would rush ahead along the path to get there, coming back to chivvy me along faster.

Red: "Come on, move quicker."
Me: "The fields aren't going to disappear in just a few minutes. Stop rushing me."

Red: "Come on, come on, come ON!"

Me: "Seriously, five minutes is not going to make any difference."

Red: "Hurry up! We're nearly there. Just two more corners!"

Me: "Yes, I know where the fields are."

Red: "Faster! I want to PLAY!"

Me: "Look, we're here. Oh, did I remember to pick up a ball?"

Red: "You do this stupid thing every single time. You and I both know you have a tennis ball in that pocket right there."

Me: "Grumpy! You mean this ball right here?"

Red: "OMG BALL! Throw it. Throw it right now. THROW THE DAMN BALL!"

Me: "Ok, ok, I've got it! Here, I'm throwing the flaming thing already!"

Red: "Wheeeee!"

Puppy: "Hello."

Red: "Wha… Oh, it's a small dog."

Puppy: "I like your tennis ball."

Red: "Human, throw the ball."

Puppy: "I'd like a ball like that."

Red: "Wheeeee!"

Puppy: "I'd really like to play with a ball like that."

Red: "Human, throw the ball."

Puppy: "Can I play with your ball?"

Red: "No. Wheeeee!"

Puppy: "But I WANT the ball!"

Red brings the ball back to me. Before he reaches me to drop the ball near my feet, the puppy (who is a black Labrador about five months old at a guess and very cute) grabs the ball from out of his mouth and runs away with it. The puppy's owner gives a shocked gasp as her pup frolics off with Red's ball.

Red: "Human! He stole my ball!"
Me: "Yes, he definitely did."
Red: "Get it back!"

It was all I could do not to dissolve into laughter, every time this happened. Red's toys were often stolen by other dogs, although this was the only time I saw the theft happen from right out of his mouth. The only reaction he ever showed was to give me a forlorn look and then wait for me to retrieve the toy or produce a replacement.

POOCH WITH POISE

Although Cass was always a very independent character, whenever we were doing anything she always liked to know what we were up to. She would often find something else to do nearby so that she could keep an eye on us, but she would also often want to 'help', whether she was actually being helpful or not. She would always definitely stick close by if we did anything involving bales of straw or hay. Ever since an altercation when we had been removing the covering from an old silage pit that had been emptied of winter feed, Cass had a hate/hate relationship with rats. On a farm, particularly when it comes to a location with warm, dark, secure sleeping spaces, rats are never very far away. They are a complete pain in bale stacks, as they chew through the strings that hold the bales together, and can make stacks unstable.

Cass: "What are you doing?"
Me: "We are moving the straw bales. There's a load with broken strings, so we're going to use the loose

stuff to start bedding down the barn for when the ewes come in for lambing. We'll stack the whole bales up again."

Cass: "Oh, I'll help."

Me: "It's fine. Cass. There probably won't be any rats showing up as they'll move away when we get close."

Cass: "Just in case, though."

Me: "If I try and send you away now, you're just going to come back and climb up the stack anyway, aren't you?"

Cass: "You know it."

Me: "Ok then, no point me trying to stop you. Let's head on up."

Cass: "Oh, I can smell them up here."

Me: "I bet you can. Just be careful. I'm not sure how stable it is right now."

Cass: "Look, I stick my head between the bales and I can really smell them well."

Me: "I'm sure you can but I'd really rather you didn't stick your head between the bales."

Cass: "I'm going right up to the top."

Me: "Cass, be careful. The straw's loose under there and the bales aren't stable."

Cass: "It's fine. Look, I'm right up at the top."

Me: "Look out! The stack's collapsing!"

I duck out of the way of the direction the bales are going to fall. As cool as a cucumber, Cass simply walks down the collapsing bale stack as if it is a perfectly normal set of stairs, hopping neatly out of the way when she reaches the ground.

Me: "Look at this mess! There's straw everywhere."

Cass: "Look on the bright side. There are definitely no rats in between the bales any more."

That was one of Cass's specialities, causing utter chaos and then casually strolling away from the epicentre, looking as if it had precisely nothing to do with her.

THE EVOLUTION OF A SPECIES

Finn has a very good line in playing the big tough hard as nails type of chap. Of course, those of us that really know him can see through it immediately as, no matter what image he tries to project, he is in fact as soft as butter and worried by many, many things. He would obviously deny that fact emphatically if he could, especially if there are others in the vicinity.

Finn: "Yay, we're out for a walk!"
Me: "Yep, it's really early, there's absolutely nobody else around and you're doing really well with the loose lead walk…"
Finn: "CAT! OMG, have to chase the cat. MUST CHASE THE CAT!"
Me: "No, no chasing the cat. We're going to carry on having a nice walk."
Finn: "I've got to chase the cat. OMG, MUST CHASE THE CAT!"
Me: "You are not chasing the cat."

Finn: "CAT! OMG, OMG, OMG, MUST CHASE THE CAT!"

Me: "Right, here's what we're going to do. You're just going to sit down while you calm down a bit for a minute because I am not going to let you chase the cat."

Finn: "But, but, but…" *sigh* "All right. Let's carry on walking."

Me: "Much better. See how nice this is?"

Finn: "Different cat! OMG, OMG, OMG, MUST CHASE THE CAT!"

Me: "Finn, you have to learn that you can't chase everything that you see. And definitely not cats."

Finn: "But I am a noble and dedicated Border Collie. Through generation after generation of intensely careful selection and breeding choices, the hunting behaviour of my ancient wild ancestors has been refined and developed. This process, happening over thousands and thousands of years, has shaped me into the perfect example of a herding breed dog. In fact, it's a real shame that I'm not in a big field of sheep right now, impressing anyone that looks on with my amazingly honed inherent genetic ability, stylish outrun and superb eye."

Me: "Finn, you're afraid of sheep."

Finn: "…Shut up."

In his defence, he has actually got past a lot of his fear with sheep now. Right up until they move into a different field, or are sheep of a different breed and therefore a different colour or anything else about them is different from what he has seen previously. Novelty is not high on his list of favourite things!

RED LORRY, YELLOW LORRY. NO, RED'S LORRY

A while after we left farming, my husband started working as a lorry driver for a company involved in the construction industry. This opened up the opportunity for Red to go to work with him and become a lorry dog. It also meant some working at weekends, which gave me the chance to ride along with them sometimes.

Red: "Why are you in the car?"
Me: "I'm coming with you today."
Red: "Oh, you're coming to the yard with us?"
Me: "That's what I said, I'm coming with you."
Red: "Ok, so this is the yard."
Me: "I have actually been here before, you know."
Red: "Don't believe you."
Me: "Yep, more than once."
Red: "You've never been here when I've been here so it didn't happen. Whatever, now you're here you have to throw the ball for me to keep me happy and

occupied while he loads the lorry. And then you can go home."

Me: "I think we may have slightly different expectations of how today is going to go."

Red: "Right, he's finished loading. You can put the ball away while he puts me in the lorry cab and then he and I can get on with our day's work."

I put the ball back in its place on the workshop shelf, wait while the paperwork for the day is all prepared and the workshop is locked up. Once this has all been done, I climb up into the passenger side of the lorry. Red is sitting on the little bed area that runs behind the seats. As I sit in the passenger seat I realise he is just staring at me.

Red: "Uh, what do you think you're doing?"

Me: "Getting comfortable in my seat before we hit the road."

Red: "Whoa! You're not coming with us!"

Me: "I'm sitting here in the passenger seat, I brought food and coffee. I'm set for the whole day with you guys."

Red: "Nobody asked ME if you could come in my lorry."

Me: "Technically it's not actually your lorry."

Red: "How very dare you! This IS my lorry and I will defend it until my dying breath."

Me: "Well we're moving now so you're stuck with me."

He subsides with less than perfect grace, giving up staring at me to lay down after a while. After a little longer he decides I might as well make myself useful while I'm there and demands that I fuss him as we are driving along the motorway, and when we pull into the services car park for a break insists that we play ball in a quiet corner. After a couple of hours, we arrive at the location where what we have transported needs to be unloaded. I settle in my seat to wait until we are ready for the off again. Suddenly there is a collie dog behind me, frantically attempting to wriggle between me and the back of the seat, and then to push me out of the seat.

Me: "HEY!"
Red: "You're in my way."
Me: "I'm just sitting in the seat here."
Red: "I need to be here. You have to move."
Me: "Ok, calm down. How about if I just shift forwards a bit so that you can get behind me?"
Red: "I suppose so if you have to sit here."
Me: "Why is it so important that you're in this seat?"
Red: "I have to supervise the unloading."

He promptly settled himself behind me and started intently staring at the side mirror of the lorry. When I looked I realised that he could actually see the unloading going on outside and was actively watching it. All loading and unloading on sites away from the home yard had to be supervised by 'the boss' in the mirror.

IF YOU CAN'T STAND THE HEAT

Cass was an excellent working dog when you had her on your side, with a real knack for getting sheep where they needed to be efficiently. Of course, sometimes it was more that she got them efficiently to where she thought they should be. There were days when you just needed to hope that she would be on your wavelength. The sheep always got to where you needed them to be, just not maybe as quickly as would be ideal.

Me: "We're all good to go, Cass. Go fetch the sheep into the pens. It's really hot up here today, so I'd appreciate it if you could bring them straight here this time."
Cass: "You will get the sheep whichever way I decide to bring them in."
Me: "It's just as hot for you as it is for the rest of us."
Cass: "Trust me, I'll be fine."
Me: "Is there any point in me arguing with you?"
Cass: "What do you think?"

Cass takes off across the field and round behind the flock of sheep, setting them running. For once, she appears to be bringing the ewes and lambs straight up to where the pens have been set up. Just before making the last little change of direction to run along the fence into the hurdles, Cass veers off. With her gone from moving them along, the sheep slow and then turn away, scattering as they head away from the pen. I watch Cass loping away across the field.

Me: "Cass, where are you going?"

Ignoring me, Cass continues until she reaches the field's water trough. Without pausing, she hops into it, laying down full length in the cool water.

Me: "What on earth are you doing? The sheep were so nearly in!"
Cass: "What? You told me to be careful because of the heat!"

Water trough hopping was always her favourite way to cool off. A quick dip and a drink all rolled into one, what could be better?

PUPPY PROTECTION INC.

Although Finn is very suspicious of people he does not know, the people that make up his circle of 'safe people' are utterly adored. Although we have carefully worked with him to make him more accepting of being left, he would far rather be with us and act as escort and personal protection at all times, given the opportunity.

Me: "I know you're comfortable laying on my feet, Finn, but I need you to move for a minute.
Finn: "Why? Where are you going? Should I come with you?"
Me: "Relax, I'm just going to see what the postman put through the front door, see if there's anything interesting in there."
Finn: "Ok, I can stay here while you do that."
Me: "All sorted. Go back to sleep now."
Finn: "Where are you going now? Do I need to come? Let me come with you."

Me: "Look, I have my glass in my hand. I'm only going to refill it because I'm thirsty. I might grab a snack while I'm out there."

Finn: "Snacks, you say? I should definitely come and help you pick snacks."

Me: "You stay there, and I'll bring you something really nice in."

Finn: "Wait, is that scraps of ham?"

Me: "Yes, yes it is. If you can stay like a good boy when I'm wandering around the house doing stuff, you get the really good snacks. Like scraps of ham."

Finn: "Huh, I think I like this."

Me: "I thought you would. See, sometimes you just don't need to go everywhere with me."

Finn: "Wait, where are you going now?"

Me: Just up to the bathroom. You can stay down here and I'll be right back."

Finn: "But what if you don't come back?"

Me: "I will definitely be back, I promise. It's not like I'm going to disappear from the bathroom. The window is too small for me to vanish through, for a start."

Finn: "But, but, but… You need a dog to protect you. It's DANGEROUS to go alone!"

I can do many things without canine protection now, but a visit to the bathroom is not on the list!

A DOG'S GOT TO DO...

This occurs one day travelling home down the farm driveway after having been out for a couple of hours. I look out of the window as we are rolling along and see the black rear end of a dog, laying contentedly in the grass, basking in the afternoon sunshine and watching over the sheep in the field as they graze. Aware of the constant concern that farmers have about livestock worrying, I carefully look at the sheep and ensure that they are showing no sign of being concerned by the dog being in with them and that the dog, from the position I am looking from, appears relaxed and not as if it is about to start chasing the stock. I reason that the person who owns the field and the sheep must have recently got himself a sheepdog.

Me: "What a lovely dog, just lying there quietly with them. Ok, Cass, I'm home. Out you come. Time to stretch your legs in the field. Cass?"

There is no sign of Cass in her shelter or run. I check all of the buildings in the farmyard, the home field and even in the house. Still nothing. Suddenly I am struck by a nagging suspicion and start walking back up the drive towards the neighbouring farmer's field.

Me: "Um, Cass? What exactly do you think you're doing?"

Cass: "I'm watching over my flock."

Me: "Yeah… Except this isn't your flock."

Cass: "There are no sheep in the field at home, so this must be my flock."

Me: "I am so glad our neighbour knows you. These are definitely not your sheep. These have brown patches in their fleeces. They don't look anything like your sheep."

Cass: "Would you believe it if I said something about dogs being colour blind?"

Me: "Not at all. How did you get out of the pen and the yard?"

Cass: "That's for me to know and you, preferably, not to find out!"

Yes, escape routes were definitely located and blocked. We were fortunate that our neighbouring farmer knew our dog and that she was not a sheep worrier, but did not intend to risk anybody else possibly coming to a different conclusion and taking the very understandable decision to protect their stock from the fear, pain and distress that livestock worrying causes.

PATIENCE BRINGS REWARDS

Dillan's prime reason for existence, as far as she was concerned, was to get as close to the nearest human being as physically possible and get plenty of fuss. As much as she loved to work, fuss and attention were definitely her ultimate goal in life, and she would always be as close as she could get.

Me: "I'm just going to stretch out on the sofa and watch this TV programme."
Dillan: "You know you'll end up falling asleep if you do that."
Me: "I don't intend to go to sleep, but it's not the end of the world if I do. Settle down and I can watch this."
Dillan: "Oh, fine. I'm just a poor neglected dog who never has any attention paid to me ever. I'll lay right here next to you, along the front of the sofa, because I'm such a loyal dog that I have to be near you at all times."
Me: "Yeah, you have such a hard life…"

I lay there watching the TV and scratching Dillan's ears for a while. I wake up about an hour later to find Dillan poised with her muzzle about half an inch away from my face.

Me: "Dillan, what are you doing?"
Dillan: "Waiting."
Me: "Waiting? For what?"
Dillan: "Well, whenever you fall asleep on the sofa for a while, there's something you usually do when you wake up. Sometimes before opening your eyes."
Me: "What's that?"

I muffle a yawn against the back of my hand.

Dillan: "That. You yawn."
Me: "So? What's so interesting about me yawning?"
Dillan: "Because if you don't open your eyes and spot me, and if I can time it just right, I'm pretty sure when you yawn I can manage to lick the roof of your mouth."

Yes, she succeeded in this. Yes, I made a LOT of disgusted noises. If there was any chance of falling asleep on the sofa, I tried to remember to wedge a cushion on the edge of the sofa to give me some kind of protective barrier!

WHOSE BED?

Roo and Red made quite the couple as they got older, and really did seem to adore each other. Together they became affectionately called 'Darby and Joan' after the proverbial old happily married couple. They were always happy to see each other, and could contentedly make themselves at home in the other's house. It was because of this ease with each other that, when my mother and sister were going away for the weekend, we offered to have Roo stay with us, and took her back to our house.

Me: "Go ahead and make yourself at home, Roo."
Roo: "Already on it. I don't know whose yoga mat this is, but it makes a great dog bed."
Me: "Yeah, I'm sure my other half will be glad you're feeling the benefit of him attempting to stretch his back out."
Roo: "Hey, he's more than welcome to come down here and join me."

Me: "Because of course, you wouldn't be scrambling all over him if he did that, right?"

Roo: "Everyone knows a little dog is going to love you, whether you actually want it right then or not."

Me: "Trust me, anyone that knows you definitely knows that fact!"

Roo: "And you all love me for it."

Me: "Yeah, you have all of us worked out pretty well."

Red: "Um, how come Roo's still here? She normally comes in for a while and then goes home."

Me: "She's staying with us tonight. Let's get the pair of you fed and happy, and then we can all relax for the evening."

Red: "Sounds good!"

We get dogs and humans fed and all settle in for a quiet evening in front of the tv. Red curls up on his bed as usual, while Roo spends her time going from sofa to sofa, alternating between cuddling up to the two human options she has to pick from.

Me: "Right, it's time for bed. You guys go out for a pee and then we'll go on up."

Roo: "Up?"

Me: "Upstairs to bed."

Roo: "But I sleep downstairs at home."

Me: "There are beds and sofas down here. You can stay down here or come upstairs."

Roo: "Oh, I'm definitely coming upstairs if that's an option."

I go through my normal bedtime routine and get into bed. As I am reading my book I get the feeling that I am being watched and turn my head to see a little brown and white face watching me.

Me: "What's the matter, Roo?"
Roo: "Where am I allowed to sleep?"
Me: "Anywhere you want. Just probably not with Red, he's not much of a snuggler at night."
Roo: "Anywhere at all?"
Me: "Sure."
Roo: "What if I want to be up there?"
Me: "What, you want to sleep on my bed? Sure."

Roo backs herself up as far as she can, then gives a cute little bum wiggle before hurling herself at the bed. I have to help her actually make it up there, as it's quite a long way up for little legs. We settle down comfortably and go to sleep. Several hours later I wake up stiff and cold. On opening my eyes I discover I am balancing on at most six inches of the mattress and have no duvet over me at all. Roo is laying at ninety degrees to me and, despite being a small dog, she is taking up almost the entire width of the double bed, and is nestled snugly in the king-sized duvet. I try to quietly wriggle further onto the bed and work some duvet loose so that I can have some warm covers.

Roo: "Hey, quit crowding me! Can't a girl get some room here?"
Me: "But you're tiny, how much room do you need?"
Roo: "All of it."

Due to one small Jack Russell, I spent the remainder of the time in bed curled up in one little corner, just to be able to get some duvet. Physically Roo may have been a small Jack Russell, but mentally I am convinced she thought she was huge!

DISTRACTION IN ACTION

Finn covers his fear of the world by acting tough. It is an evolutionary trick to avoid appearing vulnerable. Although his fears are not a funny thing, just sometimes the way in which they present and his behaviours change as a situation unfolds can be funny to watch.

Finn: "Another beautiful early summer morning walk. We just have to get across the car park here and then you can let me off the lead for a run-around, right?"
Me: "That's right, just a little further and you can run to your heart's content."
Finn: "What's that over there?"
Me: "I'm not sure, I can't quite make it out clearly yet."
Finn: "I really want to know what it is. You know I don't like strange things."
Me: "It's fine, I'm here with you. I'm not going to let anything happen to you, I promise."
Finn: "Wait a minute, is that a cat?"

Me: "I still can't see it properly yet."

Finn: "It is. It's a CAT!"

Me: "You aren't going to be allowed to chase the cat, so you might as well just walk here next to me. We'll get past the cat and into the fields, and once we're safely far enough past the cat you're not going to try and turn back, I'll let your lead off."

Finn: "No, I'm going to get the cat!"

He gets all up on his toes, bouncing and huffing and growling, doing his very best attempt to look like the perfect predatory hunting animal.

Me: "Finn, come on. You know I'm not going to let you get near that cat."

Finn: "I don't care what you say, I have to get the cat!"

The cat, a big ginger fluffy one, turns his head slowly and watches us as we draw level with him a little way across the car park. Just as Finn is beginning to really bounce on his paws and get really excitable, the cat very steadily gets up from where he's been sitting onto all four paws, puffing all of his fur up and hissing.

Finn: "Oh… Wow, look at all the seagulls over that side of the field. I think we need to go over there and have a closer look at those seagulls."

Me: "What happened to you have to get the cat over here?"

Finn: "There was a cat? I didn't notice!"

ITS VISION IS BASED ON MOVEMENT

I am in the kitchen at home, getting a head start on some meal preparation for that night. The weather has been wet, and we are all still in the process of finishing drying out from having been out following the usual morning farm routine.

Cass: "That smells good. Any of it for me?"
Me: "No, this is for us tonight. I'll feed you guys a bit later on."
Cass: "It smells REALLY good. Are you sure I can't have any?"
Me: "Yours is in the fridge. Go and sleep for a while. I'm going to be busy here for some time yet."
Cass: "Ok, I'll be in the living room then."
Me: "Not on the sofa. You're still grubby and damp on the legs from working earlier."
Cass: "I know, I know. I'll stay on the carpet on the floor."

Some little while later, I am finished getting the meal organised for that night and start to come into the living room. I hear a sudden noise, a sort of scrabbling followed by a quiet dragging sound. On peeking around the door, I see Cass, frozen in mid-slide off the sofa. Her front paws are on the floor but her back end is still on the sofa cushion.

Me: "Um, Cass? "What are you doing?"
Cass: "Oh... Nothing?"
Me: "Are you sure?"
Cass: "What's the dinosaur movie? The one with the line about being invisible if you stay very, very still?"
Me: "I think that only works on a T Rex, Cass."

That was not the only time she pulled the same trick. Every time she fell back on the 'if I don't move they can't see me' idea, even though she would obviously eventually have to move. When she did, it was always with utter confidence that nothing she could do was ever wrong. In all honesty, she was right. Who were we to argue with her?

HOW TO WIN FRIENDS ETC

One of the personality traits that Red displayed that really made him stand out was the way he behaved when around people with any kind of fear of dogs, and how he had a knack for calming them. He demonstrated his ability to get them to relax with him a number of times over the years. One of the notable examples involved the children of our next-door neighbours when we lived in town. On the first day that they saw him, both kids hid behind their parents whenever he looked at them. After a few months, things became very different.

Neighbour: "We're making some changes to our garden. The thing is it means that we need to take down this fence between the two gardens here for a while."
Me: "No problem. I'll try to make sure Red stays on our side as best as I can."

Neighbour: "Don't worry about it too much. He's a good boy, and he can't get out of our garden if he does come through, so it's not much of a drama."
Me: "I'll still do my best, but that's great to know. Just let me know if you need any help, or want to get stuff in and out through our garden rather than having to go through your house."

Work begins in the neighbour's garden and continues for a few days. The neighbour's children have been at school or nursery during the week and I have kept a close eye on Red during the evenings to make sure that he stays in our garden. At the weekend, however, I become engrossed in what I am doing and do not initially notice Red going outside. By the time I realise, he is throwing his ball around. Just as I step outside the ball goes into the bottom of next door's garden.

Me: "Red…"
Neighbour: "Leave him for a minute. He's right at the far end of the garden, so let's see what the kids do."
Boy: "Daddy, Red's in our garden."
Neighbour: "Yes, he is. He just came to get his ball back."
Boy: "Why is he throwing it around by himself?"
Me: "I've been busy today, so he hasn't really had anyone to play with today."
Boy: "He doesn't have anyone to play with?"
Me: "Not right now, no."
Boy: "Daddy, do you think I can play with Red?"
Neighbour: "You'll have to ask Jay. Red is her dog."
Me: "I'm sure Red would love for you to play with him."

The little boy collects his younger sister and they tentatively make their way down the garden towards Red.

Red: "Are they going to play with me?"
Me: "They are. Get this right and you'll be set for fun for the entire time the fence is down."
Red: "Small humans, this is the ball. You throw or kick it, and we all get to have a lot of fun. He threw the ball!"
Me: "I think I just lost my dog…"

By the time we left that house, the children who in the beginning could hardly bear to look at Red would come and knock on the door to ask for him to come out to play. A favourite game for the three of them involved Red barking at the kids, which would prompt them screaming with delight and excitement and running away. They would then come back a few seconds later to do it again, being followed by a jaunty tailed collie trotting along behind them.

ABOUT THE AUTHOR

Jay has been working with and training dogs with more enthusiasm than skill for more years than she cares to remember, largely working Border Collies (or in the case of one very determined dog, NOT working). Although no longer living on the farm or farming sheep, the Border Collie has wormed its way into her heart enough to still be the dog of choice. It was the younger of her current dogs that caused her having to research reactivity and, in the process, discover a new love of learning about dog training and behaviour. A lifelong love affair with the written word has combined with the new interest to inspire her attempt to ensure that no reactive dog owner needs to feel that they are alone.

Jay can be found in the following places:

Website: JayGurden.com
Facebook writing page: Jay Gurden @jaygurdenwriter
Facebook dog page: Blue Merle Minion @bluemerleminion
Blog: https://splodgycollies.blogspot.com/
Instagram: @jaygurden and @bluemerleminion
Twitter: @txljay

OTHER BOOKS:

Fight or Fright? A Reactive Dog Guardian's Handbook (available on Amazon worldwide):

Written by the guardian of a reactive dog and student

of canine behaviour, this book sets out to make sure that nobody in that situation has to feel alone. Packed with empathy and understanding, inside is a guide to recognising that your dog is fearful and advice to aid you in finding the help and support that you need to improve life for both you and your reactive dog. From describing how reactivity impacts on both dog and guardian physically and mentally, to guidance on finding the right kind of professional help, this book will support you on every step of the journey.

Printed in Poland
by Amazon Fulfillment
Poland Sp. z o.o., Wrocław

52314833R00085